Praise for
THE BOOK OF JOAN

"An antic, sweet remembrance of the brazen comedian."

—*Washington Post*

"Very funny."

—Cindy Adams, *New York Post*

"We have a winner. Oh yes we do. Of all the celebrity memoirs to have appeared in the last few months, we have from way back in the pack, the one that made an incredible stretch run to become the unquestioned leader. . . . If there are any smart mothers out there notable for their outspoken candor and their pop cultural literacy, Melissa Rivers' book will take care of their early summer reading needs quite nicely."

—*Buffalo News*

"Melissa Rivers offers a humorous and tender retrospective on the life and character of her mother, the late comedian Joan Rivers."

—*Publishers Weekly*

THE BOOK OF JOAN

THE BOOK OF
OF
JOAN

*Tales of Mirth, Mischief,
and Manipulation*

MELISSA RIVERS

THREE RIVERS PRESS
NEW YORK

Originally published in hardcover in the United States by
Crown Archetype, an imprint of the Crown Publishing Group,
a division of Penguin Random House LLC, New York, in 2015.

Library of Congress Cataloging-in-Publication Data
Rivers, Melissa, 1969–
The book of Joan : tales of mirth, mischief, and manipulation / Melissa
Rivers.—First edition.
1. Rivers, Joan.   2. Comedians—United States—Biography.
3. Entertainers—United States—Biography.   4. Rivers, Melissa, 1969–
5. Television producers and directors—United States—Biography.
6. Mothers and daughters—United States—Biography.   I. Title.
PN2287.R55R58 2015
792.7602'80922—dc23
[B]
2015006127

ISBN 978-1-101-90384-1
eBook ISBN 978-1-101-90383-4

PRINTED IN THE UNITED STATES OF AMERICA

Book design by Elizabeth Rendfleisch
Map by Meredith Hamilton
Cover photograph: Courtesy of the author
Insert: p. 6, bottom left: Ron Galella/Ron Galella Collection/Getty
Images; p. 7: Charles W. Bush; p. 8, top left: Charles W. Bush
All other photos courtesy of the author

10 9 8 7 6 5 4 3 2 1

First Paperback Edition

For my Mother,
whom I think about every day,

and for my Father,
who, as of this past September,
is no longer resting in peace

Contents

"Melissa, Helen Keller once said,
'Life is a great adventure, or it's nothing.' . . .
Of course, she said it to a coffee table . . . but still,
you get the point."

Borrowed Time

I NEVER THOUGHT I'd be sitting in a hospital making a decision about turning off a ventilator. I guess in my head I knew it was a possibility, as we all know we may face that kind of decision for a loved one someday. I just didn't know I'd have to make it so unexpectedly. Just last night my mother and I were on the phone, laughing and joking about an old friend she'd run into. It was a typical, checking-in-with-each-other kind of call. I had no way of knowing that it would be our last conversation.

What I *wanted* was for her to sit up and say, "Ooh, that was a nice nap. What time is hair and makeup?" What I *needed* was five minutes so I could tell her all the crazy, hilarious things that had gone on around her for the last week. We were probably the only two people in Mount Sinai who would've seen the humor in all this madness. But since I didn't get those five minutes . . .

In our family we always laughed our way through pain, so I decided to write a book that would have made her laugh. At least once a day she used to turn to me and say, "Can you believe this shit?" And I'd say, "Yes, Mommy, I can."

Mommy, I hope you're somewhere reading—and, God knows, editing—this book, but the thing I hope most of all is that you're smiling.

She Works Hard for the Money

ONE OF THE questions I'm most often asked is "Did your mother always work so hard?" I wish I had an answer. According to her cousin Alan—the only relative worth speaking to or acknowledging—"Your mother was like this before you were born. She wanted to be sure she was one step ahead of everybody else. It used to make your grandmother crazy. We'd sit down to play a game of Monopoly, and by the time we were once around the board, she'd co-op'd three hotels and was trying to foreclose on one of our cousin Charlotte's properties. I think this is one of the reasons I finally settled in Vermont. The family gatherings were way too intense for me."

My mother was a comedian, actress, writer, producer, jewelry monger, tchotchke maker, spokesperson, hand model, *Celebrity Apprentice* winner, and self-appointed somewhat-goodwill ambassador to twenty-seven Third World countries that were unaware they had a goodwill ambassador. (It was a power move on her part, not unlike the time she named herself "block captain" of her block in New York, which had no block association. (I think this was a nod to the Eisenhower years—which I never fully understood—when many suburban neighborhoods had block captains who were in charge of getting people into the local bomb shelters during nuclear attacks.) The woman was indefatigable. James Brown may have been the hardest-working man in show business, but I'm pretty sure my mother was the hardest-working woman. Even at eighty years old, she was on the go, from gig to gig, show to show, all the time. She was always working, always moving; she was like Sisyphus with jokes. A typical week for her last year was:

Monday—Start working on weekly episode of *Fashion Police* in the morning and during the day. Drive down to Philadelphia for the QVC show (and work on her new book or a TV or movie script in the car on the way down).

Tuesday—More work on *Fashion Police* and meet with her various agents, biz people, jewelry designers, etc. Nighttime performance at the West Bank Café in New York City.

Wednesday—Early morning flight to Los Angeles for *Fashion Police* meetings all day and night.

Thursday—Arrive at E! studios at 5:00 a.m. to prepare for *Fashion Police* taping at 8:00 a.m. Afterward, press obligations and business meetings. A quick dinner of Chinese food with Cooper before catching the red-eye back to New York City.

Friday—Travel to whatever city she was appearing in that night and then give a ninety-minute performance.

Saturday—Travel to whatever city she was appearing in *that* night, do *another* ninety-minute show, then travel back to New York.

Sunday—Not unlike for God, a day of rest—and by rest, I mean, reading scripts, writing a book, doing the Sunday *New York Times* crossword puzzle in ink,* and maybe, just maybe, catching the matinee of a Broadway show with her BFF, Margie Stern, and then immediately afterward calling her agent to find out if she could take over the lead in whatever show she had just seen. (I swear I once overheard her screaming at her agent, "I'd be a fabulous Willy Loman!")†

Just writing that tires *me* out.

I remember a conversation we had after one of our Very Long Thursdays—we'd shot an episode of *Fashion Police,* and then taped scenes for *Joan & Melissa: Joan*

---

* FYI, she was a terrible speller, but no matter how many spaces were allowed, she made the letters fit. No puzzle went unfinished. When I would point out that there was a mistake, she'd say, "Don't bother me with the details. It works for me." (I actually put a book of crossword puzzles, a pair of her glasses, and her favorite pens in her casket. Somewhere in heaven there's a small blonde woman misspelling a four-letter word for "Asian housemaid."‡)

† And that was a light week. She still found plenty of quality and quantity time to criticize me.

‡ The correct answer is "Amah." She's probably trying to shove in "Cashundertable."

Knows Best, and at night we did four interviews for *In Bed with Joan.* At the end of the night, after the camera crew and production team had finally left, I went downstairs to her bedroom. She was lying in bed in her bathrobe, and I started telling her that she needed to slow down. I told her that it wasn't healthy—physically, mentally, or emotionally, especially at her age—to keep working these hours. I told her that I was worried about her and Cooper was worried about her, too. I was pouring my heart out, thinking I was getting somewhere, as she hadn't interrupted me. I looked over and saw that her eyes were shut. I thought that she had fallen asleep and hadn't heard a word I'd said. So I nudged her and said, "Mom?" She shushed me and said, "Melissa, please! I'm practicing visualization techniques and I'm seeing myself as the face of Depends."

The Need to Succeed

I DON'T KNOW, or pretend to know, what happens to us after we die. Nobody really does, except the dead, and they're not talking. (At least not to me, but I have AT&T; I can barely get living people on the phone.) I also don't know if there's a heaven or hell (although I have been to Winnipeg in winter) or an afterlife. But what I do know is that if there is an afterlife, my mother is coming back as a pack animal. It's the only other one of God's creatures that was born and raised to work as hard as she did. The thing is, though, she never thought of it as work, because once she knew what she wanted to do, there was no stopping her.

I think both nature and nurture had a role to play in my mother's tireless and never-ending work ethic. Her parents were both Russian immigrants who were uprooted from their countries and came to the United States with nothing. I believe the immigrant mentality of working hard to get ahead was taught to my mother and her sister, my aunt Barbara, by their parents. So when my mother became a parent, there was no question she was going to be a working mother—and she became one long before it was fashionable or, as times have changed, necessary. Although, truth be told, she considered work a necessity, like water, air, food, and bespoke living room furniture.

She didn't have to get a job; my father always made a good salary, and we could have been more than comfortable on his income. So, during my childhood, my mother's drive was not all about money (although we certainly lived well), and it also wasn't about fame. One of her last national television interviews was on *The Tavis Smiley Show*, on July 13 and 14, 2014. Tavis asked her why she worked so hard at comedy, and she said it wasn't a choice. She told him that comedy was her calling. She said, "That's why comics are here. We were put on earth to make people laugh." Whether that's true, I don't know—I didn't take philosophy, theology, or astronomy in college—but I believe she *thought* it was true, which would explain why she took a very hard-earned and expensive degree from Barnard College in English literature and put it on a shelf in order to tell jokes to drunks at Shriners conventions.

To be totally honest, she didn't go into comedy right away. After she graduated she tried to do the "expected" thing and got a job working at the world-famous Bond Clothes in Manhattan. Her work ethic was in evidence even then, as she worked a million hours a week, doing everything and anything she was asked. Her diligence eventually paid off: she wound up marrying the boss's son, Jimmy Sanger. Her goal had been to work hard and get ahead, not get a husband, but that's what happened. Okay, truth be told, it wasn't exactly a marriage made in heaven; it was more like a marriage made in the stock room. The way the story goes—and I can't swear it's true; I wasn't there; but according to relatives who were—right after she and Jimmy took their vows and said their "I dos," my mother was standing on the receiving line and said to her cousin Alan (you remember, the one from Vermont), "Can you believe I'm doing this?" I don't know if Alan did, but she certainly didn't. Six months later she ended her marriage to Jimmy and quit her paying job at Bond.

Then she did something else nobody could believe: she went into show business. But the one thing everyone did believe was that she was going to work very hard at it.

Fly Me to the Moan

MY MOTHER WAS in show business for fifty years and she must've spent at least thirty of them traveling. She spent more time on the road than Jack Kerouac, Willie Nelson, and Aileen Wuornos combined. She had to have earned enough frequent flyer points to get 80 percent of Mia Farrow's kids first-class, round-trip tickets to Jupiter (Jupiter the planet, not Jupiter, Florida, home to the legendary Burt Reynolds dinner theater that I believe the legendary Burt Reynolds recently lost to a legendary bankruptcy court judge).

Our family was very fortunate that when we flew, we usually went first class. Anyone who tells you there's no difference between first class and coach has either never flown first class or never flown coach. For starters, in first class, while there may be the occasional whining child, there's also at least a one-in-four chance there'll be a whining celebrity, and the celebrity won't be whining because they're colicky or their ears hurt or they're bored.

They'll be whining because they've had a bad reaction to their vodka and crystal meth. They'll be sweating profusely and grinding their capped teeth into tiny ivory pegs and not understanding why one of the flight attendants won't fuck them in the bathroom.

My mother loved airplane food, so to her, first class was a five-star restaurant. She would eat her whole meal as well as mine, and anyone else's in our group. She then would ask for leftovers for her dogs. On flights with strung-out rock stars on board, leftovers were aplenty, because the stars were so busy grinding their teeth that they couldn't unhinge their jaws to put food in their mouths. My mother travelled so much that her habits became legendary—so legendary, in fact, that when I took the American Airlines red-eye from Los Angeles to New York, the flight attendants would hand *me* a bag of leftovers to bring to her for *her* dogs. I know what you're thinking: how *charming*. Yes. And her dogs weighed fourteen hundred pounds.

My mother always encouraged me to fly first class, even when I didn't have a first-class ticket (and by "encouraged," I mean "manipulated"). "Melissa, if you want to bump up to first class, don't hesitate to play the widow card." When I'd point out that I wasn't a widow, she'd tell me, "Then get a quickie marriage and kill him in his sleep. If you're on a six-hour New York–to–LA flight, it's worth a coupla years' probation to have fresh coffee, extra legroom, and warm nuts. Also, you can't steal silverware from the coach lounge because there is no coach lounge. The coach lounge is called the terminal, and it's called 'terminal' for a reason."

She also suggested that if I was "uncomfortable" playing the widow card because I wasn't actually a widow, then I should do what she did and join the Mile-High Club. Needless to say, I was appalled. My mother said, "Melissa, don't judge. Let me tell you something. Orville was much better than Wilbur, although Wilbur was quite the cuddler. Didn't you wonder how we flew all over the world all those years for free? I don't know why you're so upset; it didn't bother your father."

One of the few things my mother loved more than the first-class food on American Airlines flights was the chocolates in the American Airlines first-class lounge. She would take so many that they eventually started giving her a box every other week. All over her perfect Marie Antoinette–like apartment were little individually wrapped chocolates with "AA" labels on the wrapper. Strangers must have thought she was hosting daily meetings of Alcoholics Anonymous.

When I was little, I often went on the road with my parents, especially in the days before my mom had a regular television series. She was touring all the time, playing clubs and theaters all over the world. For me, many of those crucial formative years that make you the person you are were spent at thirty thousand feet, waiting for air traffic control to clear a runway. I was taught early on, before the age of seven, how to behave on a plane. Here are some simple, fun rules my parents gave me for plane travel:

1. Don't smoke.
2. Don't drink.

3. Don't kick the seat of the person in front of you (unless that person is smoking or drinking).

4. Don't whine, even if the plane is going down. If you're hurtling to your death at five hundred miles an hour, no one wants to hear that you didn't like the food.

5. Don't open the window and stick your head outside like a dog in a car on a freeway. This should be obvious, because if you open the window on a plane, two things will happen: (1) your head will be ripped off your body, and (2) the entire plane will decompress and drop like a rock. These events, however, will give you a chance to implement rule number four, Don't whine—which, FYI, you won't be able to do anyway, because your head's been ripped off.

6. Don't jump up and down on your seat and say, "Hey, what's that ticking sound coming from your underwear?"

One of the best pieces of advice my mother gave me was always to be kind, polite, and gracious to airline personnel no matter how rude, surly, or incompetent they are, and no matter how horrible their service may be. She said, "Remember, they're dealing with angry, disgruntled, miserable people. And then they leave home for work. Not only is your safety and well-being in their hands, but more important, so is your expensive designer luggage." She always had a thoughtful word or compliment for everyone at the airline, from the ticket agent at the counter ("You look quite snappy in that starched cotton-poly blend, low-thread-count blouse") to the pilot of the 747 ("I'll bet you haven't crashed one of these puppies in at least the last three weeks. Impressive!"). Her generosity of spirit was always appreciated, and we usually got great service. My mother once joked that if you were nice to the flight attendants on really turbulent, bumpy flights, they'd make sure you had beautiful, fur-lined vomit bags.

My mother loved flight attendants. (One of her favorite books was the 1967 bestseller *Coffee, Tea or Me,* a funny look at the lives of stewardesses, as they were known in those days. Her two other favorite books were *Helter Skelter* and *Looking for Mr. Goodbar,* which I'm sure says a lot about my mother—I just don't know what, and don't want to know.) My mother knew that flight attendants worked long hours, under difficult conditions, for very little money—all to make *her* travel experience a good one. She often referred to them as "the Saint Francises of the sky . . . except without the irritating begging and compulsive foot washing." I think she felt that, as a comic, she and flight attendants were kindred spirits because they were both trying to provide the best service they could to their customers, sometimes under difficult conditions, and often unappreciated.

She also maintained that we, as passengers, were actually spiritually connected to our flight attendants, and that "we are one," because even though flight attendants always say that "safety is our first priority," if the wings fall off the plane, we're all going to go down and perish together. The only "safety" they might provide is putting the coffee carts away so we don't get scalded before impact.

With rare exceptions (Katie Couric, Jay Leno, Pocahontas, and Ramses II) my mother liked the people she poked fun of in her act (see page 189),* which is why, back in the day, stewardesses were such a staple of her shows. Here are some of my mom's favorite flight attendant jokes:

> I was on a flight and the stewardess told me they lost my luggage. Then I see the pilot walk through the cabin wearing my dress.

> Stewardesses can be selfish. I said to one, "How do I get out if there's a fire?" She said, "If you want to be the second one off, grab my ankles."

> Stewardesses always give me a hard time. I asked one where my seat was and she said, "Two feet lower than when you were younger."

> Stewardesses can be mean. I asked one for a blanket and she said, "Would you like some hay, too?"

> They're such tramps. On most major airlines, the stewardess's call button moans when you touch it.

---

* In hindsight, I think she hated more people than she liked. She had a fake flight manifest labeled "Death Flight 5000," which had the names of all the people she hoped would be on board when the plane flew nose-first into K2. FYI, my name had been added to and scratched off her manifest so many times I could have filled the entire coach cabin myself.

Stewardesses always come on to men. "Can I get you a blanket? Fluff your pillow? How about a drink?" And this is after they get off the plane.

I asked a gay steward, "Exactly when did we leave the ground?" He said, "I don't know about you, but for me it was 1979."

Flight attendants were not my mother's only faves; she loved proctologists, too. But since this is a family book, I'm *not* going to give you a list of her favorite jokes on that topic.

My mother said that flying coach was like being on a bus with wings. And doing it with children? Puh-leeze. Very few things—including sleep deprivation, explosive colitis, and IRS audits—are as unpleasant and harrowing as flying coach with a herd of young'uns. She was right. I know; I've done it. When Cooper was six or seven his school planned a class trip to Orlando, Florida, to Disneyworld. For almost an entire day I found myself wedged in a cabin of 112 first-graders in various stages of hysteria, excitement, fear, and ants-in-the-pantsiness. The last time I experienced that level of discomfort I was stuck in an elevator in Salt Lake City with a fundamentalist Mormon Amway dealer and his wives. The flight to Disneyworld was such unremitting torture that I expected to receive a sympathy card from Louis Zamperini. Given the circumstances, I couldn't use my mother's upgrade strategies: I couldn't play the "widow card," because all the other parents knew I wasn't a widow; and I couldn't offer up a lap dance to the pilot, or else Child Protective Services would be waiting for me when we touched down at the Happiest Place on Earth. It was my own damned fault. I had ignored my mother's advice. I could have tried to give myself some breathing room by making sure that 23D remained vacant, but no, I had to be feisty and independent and disregard what I'd been taught and let whatever happened happen. I was an idiot. I should have listened to my mother when she said, "Melissa, if you want some 'me space' on the plane—and I don't care who's coming down the aisle; I don't care if it's a disabled vet or a nun with a puppy—if they try to plunk their ass down next to you, all you have to say is 'I'm a bleeder' or 'Can you believe that I've never used toilet paper?' or 'Don't worry about the sores; my doctor says once they've crusted over they're no longer contagious.' That seat will be emptier than a think tank in Mississippi."

JOAN PERRY   T E-4-516 6
6 Oxford Road
Larchmont, New York

Blonde
5'3"

COMMEDIANNE * ACTRESS *M.C.

Have played: Club Illusion inrBrooklyn
             B al Taberin in New York
             Swiss Terrace in Queens
             Hollywood in Chicago
             South Side Casino in Chicago
             Alpine Village in Cleavland

Also have starred in stright dramatic parts off Broadway in
             Driftwood.......Garrick Theatre (4 months...1958 season)
             See the Jaguar..Eli Rill Theatre (2 months..1959 season)
      have starred in comedy leads in:
             Bernardine...West Side Theatre (six Weeks..1958 season)
             Born Yesterday..Royal Theatre (2 Months...1958 season)

Have done Ivory Soap Commercial
          Parliament Commercial
          Six Month Floor Wax Commercial

Movies: Mr. Universe
        So Young, So Bad
        Ten Commandments
        North by Northwest (to be released)

Sex, Lies, and Videotape

THIS IS ONE of my mother's early headshots and résumés. I'm not sure exactly what year it's from, but I think she was on her second nose. I'm also not sure which credits were true and which projects were "in development" at this time—and by "in development," I mean "totally made up."* Finally, I have no idea why she picked the name Joan Perry. It could have been that she thought Molinsky was too Jewish, or that Perry would fit better on a marquee. Of course, it's also highly possible that she was married to someone named Perry and simply "forgot to mention it to me" over the course of the past forty-five years.

I think a lot of my mother's penchant for embellishment came as a result of being in show business. I've never met one actor or actress who, certainly in the beginning of their career, didn't lie or pad a résumé. They had to,

---

* What's also interesting is that she failed to mention to me that she'd worked with Hitchcock!

since most of them had day jobs as waiters—and serving waffles at IHOP isn't going to help get you a role on *The Young & the Restless.*

Her theory about lying on résumés? "Who really calls and checks?" She figured if she got caught, she'd just say, "I got cut from the movie" or "I wound up on the cutting room floor due to time." She was the human Wikipedia; a lot of what was on her original résumés wasn't true, but it sure sounded good.

She once pointed out that Kurt Waldheim, former president of Austria and UN secretary general, never mentioned that he was a guard in a Nazi concentration camp. "Melissa, nowhere on Kurt Waldheim's résumé does it say, '1938 to '41: Gassed the Weinbergs.' If he can lie on his résumé and become head of the UN, who'll care that I didn't really work with Brando?"

Death Be Not Loud

The existence of death actually heightens life and
makes it something to be savored every minute.

—JOAN RIVERS
From Mother to Daughter

Y MOTHER HAD a lifelong obsession with death. I don't
mean a mild obsession. I mean a deep-seated, get-up-
in-the-middle-of-the-night-with-heart-palpitations
obsession, the kind that needs to be treated by a psychiatrist, not a psychologist (they can't write prescriptions) or
a social worker (they can't even call a psychologist to get
him to call a psychiatrist to write a prescription). She was
obsessed with her death, my death, and random friends'
deaths—in short, everybody's.

When I was growing up, each morning before my
father went to work and I went to school, we'd all sit
in the kitchen having breakfast and my parents would
read the newspaper. My father would read the business

section, the main section, and the entertainment section. My mother would read the obituaries and the—wait. There's no "and." The obituaries were all she'd read. She was fascinated by who'd died, and how, and were there survivors, and was there a will, and had they left a nice apartment with a view that she could get a good deal on?

She actually created a game we'd play at the table. It was a variation on the "if you eat your vegetables, I'll put a piece of candy in your lunchbox" game. The payoff was the same, but the setup was different. My mother would read part of an obituary in the paper, and I'd have to guess facts about the deceased. For every fact I got right, I'd get a KitKat or a gummy bear. For example, she'd read, " 'Margaret Luanne Whiteman, eighty-seven. Spent sixty years volunteering at the local women's Rotary Club. Had nine children and fourteen grandchildren.' What do we know about Maggie?" The answers of course were: (1) she's from the Midwest or the South, because no East or West Coast city person would name a child Luanne; and (2) she's not Jewish, because Jews don't do Rotary Clubs or have nine children. ("Think of the stretch marks!") She stopped playing the game when I was twelve because I'd gotten so good at it she was afraid I'd develop diabetes.

Most parents send their children off to school with little bromides like "Have a great day! I can't wait to see you later!" or "Do your best at school today. We're having your favorite pizza for dinner tonight!" My mother would send me off with "Enjoy yourself. We could all be dead tomorrow." How uplifting. (Things didn't change over time, either. As recently as last year we had exchanges like "Melissa, do you have supplies in the house, so when disaster strikes or the terrorists land on the beach in Malibu, you're prepared?" "Mom, what are the odds terrorists are coming to Malibu?" "You never know. They could have boats.")

I never fully understood her death obsession because I'm, well, normal. The things I obsess about tend to fall within normal parameters, i.e., work, Cooper, school, and the size of my ass.

When I was in high school I asked her why she was so worried about death. She said, "I just want to make sure that when Daddy or I die, the insurance companies don't fuck you."

I said, "Really, that's where your mind goes?" She said, "Yes, of course. Doesn't everyone's?"

Well, probably not everyone's, but I guess my father's mind went there, too. Yet, unlike my mother, he wasn't worried about terrorists washing up on shore, or Armageddon. He was worried about what happened afterward—and sadly, with good reason.

Unbeknownst to us, before he committed suicide, he had our estate and finances planned, not only for that moment in time but for the future as well, so that in either of our lifetimes, there would never be a trap door we could fall through. He literally laid out for us how to deal with, handle, and manage both our business and family finances. He was meticulous and precise, and dotted every *i* and crossed every *t*. And thank God he did, because after he died, my mother was at a total loss. She had no idea what to do or where to turn. My father had run the business; all she had had to do was be funny. She had no clue about finances or mortgages or college funds; she didn't even know where he kept the house keys. In spite of the fact that she was a world-famous celebrity, there was an old-fashioned underpinning to their real relationship, and at home her job wasn't to be Joan Rivers; her job was to be Mrs. Rosenberg, and Melissa's mom.

As devastating an event as my father's death was, years later I discovered I'd taken something positive away from it. After Cooper was born, it became time for me to draw up my first will. When it was finished, it turned out to be a virtual copy of the plan my father had set out for my mother and me.

My father's plan (implemented by Michael Karlin, who has been our business manager for thirty years—and is Cooper's godfather) helped in many ways, particularly when my mother was left to her own devices. Here's an example: For as long as I can remember, once a week she would be given petty cash by her assistant, who had withdrawn it from the bank, so she wouldn't be walking around with just a credit card and a wallet full of ones. My mother would take the cash, put half in her pocket, and stash the other half in drawers and other secret hiding places in her bedroom. She would do this for weeks and weeks on end. (Sometimes, just to cheer herself up, she would lock herself in her room with the stash and count it!) Then, when she had hidden away enough, she would go purchase something (shoes, fur coat, diamond necklace, etc.) that "Michael Karlin can't stop me from buying, or tell me I can't afford! He doesn't have to know."

Once, after one of her clandestine shopping sprees,

Michael called and asked me a question he'd been dying to ask since my father passed away: "Does your mother realize that I still know exactly how much she spends and how much she hides because the cash she withdrew came from her account, and I run the account? I've been aware of this game for years, but I know it makes her happy to think she's getting away with something, so I let her sneak around and squirrel and spend."

Knowing that this was her way of operating when it came to money, after she died I had to shake out every book, magazine, and folder; look for false-bottom drawers; unscrew aerosol cans and dig through cereal boxes, looking for cash she had secreted away. I think the grand total of what I uncovered was four hundred seventy-three dollars, mostly in fives and ones, and the occasional crumpled-up twenty. I've saved that stash, and on her birthday I'm going to go out and buy something fancy and not tell Michael Karlin.

"Here's Johnny...!"

I N 1965 MY mother made her first appearance on *The Tonight Show* with Johnny Carson. She was so funny that, at the end of her segment, Johnny said to her, on the air, "You're going to be a star."

Back then the entertainment world was very different—Egads! No cell phones?—and there was no such thing as an "overnight success." Up until the creation of YouTube (e.g., Justin Bieber) and the mass-marketing of sex tapes (Do I have to tell you?), performers who got a big break had put in years and years of work before they became "overnight sensations." My mother once said, "Up until social media the only way to become a household name overnight was to kill your parents. No one ever heard of Lyle and Erik Menendez until they had a bad Tuesday and got a little annoyed with Mom and Dad. Then suddenly—BOOM! The next morning, they're the most famous couple since Sonny and Cher."

It took my mother years to become an overnight sensation. She auditioned for *The Tonight Show* seven times and was rejected by the bookers seven times. One night a comedian who shall remain nameless—I'm not protecting him; I just don't know who it was—was on *The Tonight Show* and bombed as bad as Hiroshima. Bill Cosby, who had just become one of Johnny's favorite guests (and had started out with my mother), watched the show that night and called the bookers and said, "You'll book *that* guy, but you won't book Joan? How much worse could she possibly do?" So they relented and booked her. In those days there were only three television networks, and everybody watched *The Tonight Show*. When you appeared on it, you became instantly recognizable, especially if you did well. My mother told me that the day after she did *The Tonight Show,* she went to the bank and asked them to hold a check she couldn't cover. The teller, who had obviously seen her on TV the night before, said, "Don't worry, Miss Rivers. We know you're good for it."

The second big thing that came out of her first appearance on *The Tonight Show* was my father. Edgar Alfred Rosenberg was a producer in New York and was looking for a writer to punch up the script for a movie he was producing. A friend of his suggested this funny girl he had just seen on *The Tonight Show*. As fate would have it, my mother was working in town that night, so my father and his friends went down to the Village to see her perform at the Bitter End. He liked what he saw, and set up a meeting. Apparently the meeting went well. Not only did he hire her, but five days later he married her! Clearly my father was the original multitasker.

I know what you're thinking: Five days? Who gets married after five days? That's what I thought, too, once

I was old enough to realize that "speed engagements" weren't normal. I must've been around fifteen, and we were all having breakfast at home one morning when I decided to bring the subject up with my parents. I was chatting with my mother—my father was trying to ignore us, as any man with a belligerent teenage daughter does— and I asked her, "Why did you and Daddy get married so fast? Were you pregnant? Is there an older sibling I don't know about?" She put down her bagel and said, "Melissa, we just knew. It wasn't love at first sight for either of us. There were no fireworks or lightning bolts. It wasn't some great romance like Hepburn and Tracy. We both just knew. We had the same sense of humor, the same values, and we wanted the same things out of life. And if you ever try and run off and get married in five days your father will kill you."

Back to business. Let's review:

1. Johnny gave my mother her big career break.
2. Because she was on *The Tonight Show*, she met my father.
3. Because she met my father, she had me.
4. Because she had me, you're reading this book.

How do you say thank you to someone who's responsible for all that? Nine months after I was born, my parents came up with the perfect thank-you gift. For Johnny's birthday they dressed me up and had the nanny hand-deliver me to *The Tonight Show* offices. They'd attached a note that read, "We wanted to thank you for everything you've done for us, so we've sent you our most prized possession, our daughter, Melissa. FYI, she doesn't like Brussels sprouts; they make her windy."

I've been told that Johnny held me in his arms during an entire script meeting before giving me back to the nanny, who returned me to my parents. Everybody had a good laugh but me; I was too busy developing abandonment issues.

Truth Be Told

If you tell the truth, you don't have to remember
anything.

—MARK TWAIN

M Y MOTHER REMEMBERED everything; she had to. The
woman loved to lie. Her relationship with the truth
was like Jennifer Aniston's relationship with Angelina Jolie—they weren't close. I mentioned the "lying
thing" to my mother once, and I even brought up the just-
cited Mark Twain quote. Her response? "Where's Mark
Twain today? Dead, that's where. Show's what the fuck
he knew."

Now, when I say she liked to lie, I don't mean she lied
pathologically, or told huge lies of global importance. It
wasn't like when Bill Clinton wagged his finger in the
camera and denied wagging his schlong in Monica Lew-
insky, or when Dick Cheney lied and said that waterboarding wasn't torture, but just "freshening up."

To be fair, I think *lie* is an awfully strong term for what my mother did, because when she "circled around the truth," she wasn't doing it to hurt anyone, and if she did hurt someone, she would be mortified. That said, would she lie to get the upper hand in an argument, or to put herself in an advantageous business position? Absolutely. Would she do it to keep something private that shouldn't be public? Absolutely, but who wouldn't? (My mother told me that, in reality, world-class altruist Princess Diana hated hugging the lepers in Africa, and that the only reason she did so was because it gave her cover for the fact that she and the boyfriend had a secret fuck pad in the Serengeti. Of course, I have no way of knowing if that story was true.)

Here are some terms I much prefer to use to describe my mother's creative ways with the truth:

- Embellish
- Modify
- Adjust
- Interpret
- Reinterpret
- Fudge
- Blur
- In the neighborhood
- Close enough
- Tinkering with facts
- Not totally accurate
- Completely made up
- Factually adjacent
- You're shittin' me, right?

Most of my mother's fibs were simply embellishments to make a story she was telling better or more interesting. "Melissa, why bore people if you don't have to? Leave that to Katie Couric."

For example, a few years ago, when my mother was on tour in Canada, she had a three-hour flight from Toronto to Winnipeg. She always called me after her flights landed, so I'd know she'd arrived safely. Sure enough, she calls me and tells me she's arrived in Winnipeg. She then tells me the flight was delayed due to gale-force headwinds blowing in from the polar ice caps, that the plane had pitched and dropped—she thinks they hit a flock of geese—that passengers were being tossed around, and that it was a miracle they landed safely. Her assistant, Graham, who was travelling with her, told me that the skies were clear, the plane hit an air bump once, and the only tossing my mother did was in her sleep, once her Ambien kicked in. He said the miracle was that the flight was twenty minutes early and the airport actually had a gate ready and waiting for them. When I called my mother on her shit, I said, "Mom, why did you make all that up and make me nervous?" She said, "If I'd told you it was a simple, easy flight, would you have found it interesting?" I said, "No." She said, "My point exactly. If I'd told you the truth, you would've clicked over and answered call waiting."

The irony is that when she actually did need to lie, as practiced as she was, she was a terrible liar. Last July, she wanted to get out of going to a dinner she was invited to at some agent's house in Beverly Hills. Normally when she felt the need to duck out of a commitment like that, she'd make up some complex, multipronged, multilayered story (often involving gunplay or a carjacking), a lie in which she would, without fail, get caught. So I told her, "Mom, tonight, if you're not going to tell the truth, that you're just simply too tired to go out and would rather stay home and watch Investigation Discovery's new episode of *Who the (Bleep) Did I Marry?*, then why don't you just keep the lie simple? Just tell them you're not feeling well, that you had bad shellfish for lunch? It's happened to everybody, and nobody wants to hear the details."

So she calls. She tells them she had bad shellfish. Then she tells them the name of the restaurant she ate at; the fact that her waiter, Barry, couldn't have been nicer; that she had trouble getting a cab so she'd called Uber; and that on her way home in her Uber car she'd puked in her purse, which really upset her driver, Mustafa. And even though she knew the tip was included, she gave him an extra ten for the trouble.

Then she hung up. I said, "What part of 'simple' did you not understand? Now you're going to get caught in the lie." She looked me dead in the eye and said, "I think they believed me." I said, "Trust me, they didn't. Again I just don't understand why you didn't tell the truth." She said, "Because the truth would not have been interesting. Now, shhhh; my show is starting."

One of her favorite games was answering the phone in a foreign accent, in case it was someone she didn't want to talk to. Unfortunately, she wasn't very good at accents; nor did she ever think she had a recognizable voice. Even Marlee Matlin would have recognized that lilting tone. It was certainly not the sound of tinkling bells or a peaceful, babbling brook. She also couldn't keep the accent straight to one country. "Bonjour. 'Allo? No, Meez Rivers. She no ccchhome." Then, once she realized it was someone she actually wanted to talk to, she'd drop the accent and go, "Oh, hi! So, anyway . . ."

Movin' on Up!

IN 1993, GLORIA Steinem and the Ms. Foundation created the national Take Our Daughters to Work Day, and parents all across America started taking their daughters to their offices with them. A wonderful thing, but the start of a movement? Not really; my mother was doing that in 1973. And she wasn't taking me to her office; she was taking me to Las Vegas.

Early in her stand-up career my mother played Las Vegas thirty weeks a year, and I got a behind-the-scenes view of all the big stars she opened for—and she opened for everyone. I could list all their names here, but it would be easier just to list the people she didn't open for: Frank Sinatra, Elvis, Liberace, and the Rat Pack (and that's only because they predated her). She did have her regulars, though: Mac Davis, Neil Sedaka, Tony Bennett, Barry Manilow, Sergio Franchi, Bobby Vinton, Tony Orlando (with and without Dawn), Glenn Campbell, Engelbert Humperdinck, John Davidson, Tom Jones, Shirley Mac-Laine, Helen Reddy, and the Mamas and the Papas (after

Cass Elliot died and they replaced her, creating the Step-mamas and the Papas), and Lola Falana.*

My mother referred to herself as the Strip Slut because she'd peddle her wares at every hotel on Las Vegas Boule-vard. After she'd close on Sunday night at Caesars Palace, we'd go back up to our room, pack our bags, and schlep across the street to the Sands, where she'd start working on Monday. I remember standing in the huge, sweeping hotel driveway watching her name come down on one marquee and go up on another. Years later, when she was a headliner, I was so excited and proud the first time I saw her name on the top of the marquee, in the big, fancy let-ters. I said, "Mommy, look how big your name is! What does that mean?" "It means we get free room service and a bigger dressing room." She wasn't totally kidding. She once told me, and reiterated it for the rest of her life, "As a performer, no matter how big you get, you always enter and exit through the kitchen." This quote has been at-tributed to Jack Benny. She would always follow it up with "Missy, never forget—to the public, I'm famous, but to the casino owners, I'm just the hired help."

She was right. Las Vegas is *all* about casino money. The hotels and casinos don't want their shows to go on for longer than ninety minutes because "time, literally, is money."

One night my mother was rocking the house and was

---

* Lola Falana insisted on being known as the First Lady of Las Vegas. So, every night onstage, she was introduced as "Lolafalana-thefirstladyoflasvegas." Repeat it often enough and it has a magical tone and small creatures might just appear at your door!

having such a good time that she ran five minutes over. The next day, she received a phone call asking if she knew that for every minute she ran over, it cost the casino two hundred thousand dollars. She was then asked if she thought she was a million dollars' worth of funny. From that night forward, she always wore a watch onstage and had a big clock visible off in the wings.

By the time I was six, I'd clocked more hours in Vegas than a Mafia bagman. I think our family single-handedly kept Western Airlines afloat—"Western Airlines, the *only* way to fly!"—shuttling us back and forth from Los Angeles to Las Vegas. While other first-graders were in school learning to add and subtract, I was at a blackjack table learning whether or not to hit on a hard sixteen. No one believes this, but before I could even recite the Pledge of Allegiance, I could recite my mother's act, which made me very handy when she hadn't performed in a while and was worried about being rusty. While she was in her makeup chair in the dressing room before the show, she'd have me sit on the edge of the bathtub and recite her act to her. To this day, if I had to, I could still give you a tight twenty. ("First wife, when you die, have all your jewelry buried on you. If the second one wants it, let the bitch dig for it.")

I also somehow retained all the aforementioned stars' acts, which made for a very clever party trick. You haven't lived until you've heard a four-year-old do twelve minutes on going to the gynecologist; follow it with an a cappella version of "Copacabana," with the backup parts included; and close with "In the Ghetto." (For those of you who don't know, Mac Davis wrote that song for Elvis, and Elvis allowed Mac to perform it in his act. I know because I could sing it.)

This year, at Clive Davis's famous pre–Grammy Awards party, I ran into Barry Manilow. He and my mom had been friends for years and had even worked together in the Greenwich Village nightclubs in New York City, when they were both starting out. Barry and I chatted for a few minutes, and then I told him I could still do his act for him. And if I'd had ninety minutes, I would have. But given that we were at a party and not a concert hall, he had to settle for my abbreviated version of his famed commercials medley. I don't know if he was flattered or horrified, but either way, it was a fun moment for both of us.

Las Vegas was and is a 24/7/365 town, so a lot of days, nights, and even holidays were spent with the children of all the other stars who were performing there at the time. Backstage at hotels was our playground. Steve Lawrence and Eydie Gormé's kids were always in charge because they were the oldest. I hung out with the Vintons' kids, Neil Sedaka's kids, and with Chastity Bono, just to name a few. We always wondered why Liberace had never had kids; he was such an outgoing fella.

If you wanted to know what was going on in Las Vegas, all you had to do was tap into the Kid Mafia. We knew who was doing what and to whom. Not only did we know where to find the best game rooms and arcades, but we also knew the swimming pools with the most permissive lifeguards, who would let us jump in from the high dive. We even had the skinny on the *original* Siegfried and Roy scandal, back in the day when they were in a variety show and one of their big cats was accused of eating a member of the dog act. (I would tell you what actually happened, but on the advice of my mother, Dead Men Don't Wear Plaid . . . wait, that's not it; it's something about loose lips and a shallow grave in the desert.)

The MGM Grand hotel used to have a great movie theater that ran a different classic film each week. It was one of our favorite Kid Mafia hangouts—not because we were such huge fans of *Gone with the Wind* or *The Little Dictator,* but because the theater was across the hall from the arcade and the candy store. Our parents thought we were checking out Peter O'Toole and Charlie Chaplin when in fact we were checking out Donkey Kong and Red Vines. One time I had a loose tooth that I was working with everything I had. I knew that if it came out I'd have arcade money for the next day. So I snuck into the movie theater and enlisted one of Abbe Lane's sons to help me pull the tooth out. We waited until the big, weepy death scene in *Dark Victory* and . . . yank! There was blood everywhere, but it was worth it. The blood trail led my mother to believe I was at the movies, and Bingo! The next day I had enough money for all my friends to play video games and develop sugar highs!

I spent a lot of holidays and birthdays in Las Vegas. Christmas in Las Vegas was a little confusing. I remember once I asked my mother why the showgirl sitting on Santa's lap was giggling and making Santa so happy and out of breath? She said, "Don't ask. Pretend it's a car accident and look away."

On my eleventh birthday I had an experience that

I'm pretty sure most other kids never had. My mother was headlining in Las Vegas and the Village People were opening for her. On their way to the stage, some of them (the Cowboy, the Indian Chief, and the hairy guy in the assless chaps) popped their heads into the dressing room to say, "Happy Birthday" and give me a present. I got their latest album; my mother's hairdresser got a date. In Las Vegas, everybody wins.

Can I Take Your Order, Please?

> Melissa, according to a man I once knew, who shall
> remain nameless—let's call him Not Your Father—
> room service is like a blow job; even when it's bad,
> it's good.
>
> —JOAN RIVERS

I'M GOING TO assume that most of you reading this book
have, at some point in your lives, stayed in a hotel and
ordered room service. (For those who haven't, I'm going
to guess that's because either you're in the Witness Protec-
tion Program and spend most of your days moving from
safe house to safe house, or you have a highly contagious
disease and are not only housebound but also swaddled in
Saran Wrap like the Boy in the Plastic Bubble.*)

---

* *The Boy in the Plastic Bubble* was a TV movie starring John Tra-
volta, about a boy who had to live inside a plastic bubble† because he
couldn't be exposed to germs. Needless to say, he was never able to
get a job working in the kitchen of a Korean restaurant.
† A plastic bubble is a large, transparent, incubator-like structure.

My mother loved room service almost as much as she hated cooking. ("If God wanted me to cook, he would have made my hands aluminum.") She believed that room service was God's apology to the Jews for our having to spend forty years wandering the desert and living on a diet of matzoh and camel dung. (At Passover my mother used to amend the Bible stories to conform to her version of history. "Melissa, how much did God love us? For forty years we lived on unleavened bread, which is terribly binding, yet if you check out the photos from those days, all the Jews were thin. Not a bloated salesman or hippy housewife in the bunch. How does that happen? It's a miracle, that's how. Thank you, God. Amen.")

Just as they did with towels, linens, and soaps, *mi madre y padre* figured out how to game the room service system. Room service used to charge by the number of setups (that's why they ask you how many people it is for), so they'd hide some of the setup from the morning meal and use them for later. They'd make me drink cereal from a glass, so we'd have two forks and a knife left over for lunch. By the end of the week, they were paying us to eat in.

Starting at the age of five, no matter what city or what kind of hotel we were in, I always had to "dress" for room service, as though I were dining in a five-star restaurant. I thought this was stupid, so one night, in one of my argumentative moods, I snapped at my mother, "Why the hell do I have to dress up for room service? This is ridiculous. Who's going to see me?" She jumped all over that one. "The waiter, Melissa, that's who. There's a fifty percent chance he's single and sixty percent chance he's straight. You're not getting any younger. Play the odds, dress up!" I said, "Ma! Are you serious?" She said, "Yes, I am. You don't know, his father might own this hotel, and you're going to blow the chance at living on an estate and owning a yacht because you're too lazy to get out of your holey sweat pants."

And you wonder why so many children of celebrities drink.

Once my mother's career had taken off, we stayed only in hotels that had twenty-four-hour room service. Quite reasonable, considering she sometimes didn't come off-stage until 11:00 p.m., and after doing meet and greets, and signing autographs, we often didn't get back to our hotel until after 1:00 a.m. Even on days off between shows, we'd order room service late at night. I think in part because our body clocks were timed to my mother's performance schedule. We were used to eating late, like they do in New York or Paris or Spain. (In New York, cooking is an anomaly; in fact, really smart landlords list the oven as a "quaint second bedroom" and jack up the rent another thousand dollars.)

I think the other reason my mother liked to order food late was because she couldn't stand people who ate dinner really early. She once said, "You know who eats dinner early, Melissa? Children, old people, Christian farmhands, and prisoners, that's who. Now go call your father and tell him dinner's at eight."

My parents felt there were never enough lamps in hotel rooms, so my mother would call down to the front desk or the concierge and ask for an extra lamp. (She made those calls, not my father. Apparently the two of them decided that her voice was far more intimidating than his. In hindsight, I concur.) Invariably, her request would be denied, usually with a brusque "We have no extra lamps." And she'd reply, in an equally brusque tone, "Are you telling me that if the president of the United States came to this hotel and asked for an extra lamp, you wouldn't get him one?" The concierge would say, "No, we'd find one." And she'd say, "Well, I promise you he's not coming; you can safely give me that lamp."

A Sport by Any Other Name

Circa 1984

    Me: Mom, I want to join the volleyball team.

    Joan: Jews don't play sports.

    Me: I'm Jewish; I play sports.

    Joan: You were adopted.

    Me: I was *not*.

    Joan: Jews don't play sports; they own sports franchises.

WHEN I WAS growing up in California we belonged to a country club, where my parents would spend lazy summer days having cocktails, playing cards with friends, and swimming in the gene pool, which is the only pool they would have gone in, because they were not exactly what one would call "sportsmen." My mother was so nonathletic that when she was in high school the gym teacher excused her from class without her even asking—for the entire year. When it came to sports, not only was she disinterested, she was totally illiterate. For someone who made a living on her command of the English language, I found it remarkable that she couldn't keep straight the difference between a touchdown and a knockout. Here's the extent of her knowledge of sports: Joe DiMaggio married Marilyn Monroe—and Marilyn could've done a lot better. The only athletic endeavor my mother participated in was power shopping, and during holiday sales, she turned it into a contact sport.

My father was no better; he was so nonathletic that the local college wouldn't let him be the team accountant, even though he had a master's degree in accounting—and he was only in the third grade. But my father *was* a sports fan. One of my fondest memories of him is lying on my parents' bed, just the two of us, watching football, while my mother is downstairs loudly ordering things on his credit cards.

Yet I am very athletic, which should prove to all "science deniers"—are you listening, all of you batshit crazy nutbags on the science committee in Congress?—that Darwin had a point and recessive genes *do* exist, although I am not stating for certain that that's the case here. (FYI, my mother loved recessive genes. We'd be walking down the block and she'd notice a family across the street and she'd say, "Missy, is there anything better than seeing a really good-looking couple pushing a baby that looks like a Sasquatch who got caught in a house fire? I think not.")

Of all the types of children my parents could have had, they never would've expected, or wanted, an athletic one. Asian? Yes. Seven feet tall? Possibly. Conjoined twins? A delicious maybe. But athletic? Not in a million years. My mother looked at sports the way Liberace looked at women—the outfits might be interesting, but the rest of it was boring and useless.

Since my athleticism and love of sports couldn't be proven through heredity—on the combined Rosenberg/Molinsky family tree there was not one ancestor who was known for running, kicking, or tackling, and the only things they threw were tantrums—my mother couldn't figure out how or why I'd become interested in sports. From as early as anyone can remember, I liked athletics. As a baby, I jogged before I could walk. In kindergarten, all my friends liked to watch *Mister Rogers' Neighborhood* and *Sesame Street*; I was hooked on NASCAR's Firecracker 400 from Daytona Beach.

For a few years when I was in high school, my mother was convinced that the only reason I was playing sports was because I was trying to gently break the news to her that I was a lesbian. When that didn't pan out, she figured I was simply doing it out of spite.

I think her lack of interest in sports came from the fact that she was not a terribly coordinated person. When did you ever hear anyone say, "My God, that Joan Rivers glides across the floor like a gazelle?" She was so uncoordinated she could actually stub a knee. She couldn't dance; she had absolutely no rhythm. Even *Dancing with the Stars,* a show that books people with no legs, never invited her on. Apparently the contestants with missing limbs could at least find the beat.

By the way, it's not that she didn't *want* to go on *Dancing with the Stars*. It's just that she knew her limitations. Yet she never let those limitations stop her. One day she called me with what she described as a "genius plan" to get on the show, in spite of her inability to channel Twyla Tharp. She wanted the network to book us as a team. Here's the plan: She would do all the easy steps. Then, when the routines became more difficult, I would run in, in a matching outfit, take her place and do the kick, spin, or whatever the more complicated move was, and then run out. "Melissa, it's fantastic! No one's ever done it before." When I replied, "There's a reason for that. I want no part of this," she mumbled something about my being impossible to work with and hung up the phone.

One winter we took a vacation to Vail, Colorado, and my mother tried to ski, but she was afraid of heights, which made the chairlift a problem. She gave it one shot, fell down, and that was it. (Of course, she fell on a hill that was so low it had no chairlift.) After that, she just sat in the lodge "encouraging" the other skiers with cheers of support like "Get off that bunny hill, you big wuss," and "Don't be such a hotdogger!" And that was just to the four-year-olds in the pre-K group.

I'm not suggesting that because my mother didn't like athletics she didn't take care of herself. She did work out. She walked on the treadmill, she lifted light weights, and she even hired a trainer. Of course, the second the trainer arrived, she'd bamboozle him by sitting and having a cup of coffee with him first, feigning interest in his steroid-riddled life, and then suddenly—it's snack time and, Holy Cow! Before you know it, she's got only five minutes on the treadmill and the trainer has to leave to wax his chest and put on his man tan.

My mother stayed in shape by doing one of the two

physical things she was good at: walking; the other was shopping. She walked everywhere. Mind you, she couldn't walk six feet in sneakers—actually she could, but she didn't want to; she didn't like sneakers; she didn't believe they were flattering to the leg—but she could hotfoot it from Saks to Bergdorf in under four minutes in a pair of heels. And even though she never set foot in a gym unless she was paid to do a show there, she nonetheless gave me advice on the subject: "Melissa, always wear full makeup when you go to the gym; you never know whom you're going to meet. They can't *all* be gay." Similarly, when I'd go out to play tennis, she's say, "I know you have a good serve, but a little lipstick wouldn't hurt you."

To be fair, I'll concede that she did attend sporting events periodically, but that's only because she was friendly with the owners. (She actually turned down Lakers courtside season seats because "Why would I want to sit so close that all these giant players would sweat on me? Ucch.") I remember after one New York Jets football game, in which they got clobbered, my mother went up to her friend, the owner, Woody Johnson, to thank him for inviting us and to give him a piece of advice. She told him that, in her opinion, the cheerleaders needed sexier uniforms. She didn't care that it was freezing outside. If the girls looked hotter, no one would care that the team lost.

There *was* one sporting event she did enjoy attending, and that was the Kentucky Derby. That's because she got to wear a hat, the jockeys wore pretty colors, and she could drink.

My mother didn't fail at many things in life, but being

a sports mom was one of them. I give her credit because she tried, but it wasn't easy because (a) she didn't like sports, and (b) she didn't like children, and youth sports are filled with them. On the food chain of things she liked, sports ranked about the same as dysentery. (She actually preferred dysentery over children, because if you have it, you can at least lose weight.)

She (and my father) came to all my sporting events even if the results weren't what you'd call optimal. When I was in fifth grade, I was on the school swim team. Before every meet, my parents brought Toblerone chocolate for all the kids; they seriously thought the sugar rush would help us swim faster. Needless to say, we didn't win a lot: we were so bloated and cramped we were lucky we didn't drown. Apparently the "Don't Eat an Hour before Going in the Water" memo never caught my parents' attention. Yet in spite of the mounting losses, my mom and dad were the most popular parents on the team. "Oh, look, it's the Rosenbergs. Yay! Can we have some chocolate?"

My favorite sport growing up was horseback riding, and I competed in a lot of equestrian events. As I've said, my parents made a valiant effort to be good sports parents—in fact, too much of a valiant effort. They always showed up, and I mean *always*. They were there for every event, every practice, and every grooming session. It was embarrassing—not because of their constant presence but because, in all the times they were there, they never learned anything. They were so uninformed that I finally said, "Either learn a little bit or don't come. It's becoming humiliating. After twenty years of my riding, you should at least have *accidentally* picked up some of the rules. At least the one about not making startling noises near the horses!"

One would have thought that with all the time my parents spent traipsing to games, meets, and horse shows, they would at least have been interested in the results. Nope. They couldn't have cared less. Turns out my mother was frequently asleep behind her oversize sunglasses, and managed to stay upright only by propping herself against my father, who would usually be listening to a business report on his Walkman radio. As an adult, I asked her, "If it was such torture, why were you and Daddy there?" She shared with me that one of her pediatricians once told her that while "quality time" with a child was important, so was "quantity time," so even if she didn't care or was bored shitless by the event, she'd show up.

Looking back, I see that what embarrassed me as a teenager I've taken to heart as an adult: the "quantity time" she gave me is one of the reasons I'm so involved with Cooper. Unlike my mother, I actually love, appreciate, and enjoy the sports he plays. I can even tell you what sport it is, how it's played, and what the rules are. Last year, my mom and I were at one of Cooper's lacrosse games and I was screaming and yelling at the top of my lungs. She looked at me, with disdain and horror, and said, "Oh my God! You've become one of them! This *really* matters to you? Where did I go wrong, and please God, tell me that's not a jersey you're wearing!" FYI, whenever my mother went to one of Cooper's games, she wore her "uniform": black pants, black top, jacket, low heels, and jewelry. It's the dead of summer at an outdoor lacrosse tournament, and she's Johnny Cash. She would also be in full makeup and hair. Why? Because she didn't want any eighth-grade kid to go back to his parents and say, "I saw Joan Rivers; she didn't look good."

When we went to Cooper's lacrosse games, I enjoyed watching my mother almost as much as I enjoyed watching Cooper—because she knew nothing about lacrosse. She just clapped whenever anyone else clapped, even if it was against our team. She followed the crowd like a lemming off a cliff. Seeing my mother clapping with all her heart, even though she didn't have a clue what she was clapping for, made me realize that while she may not have been the stereotypical, drawing-board sports mom, she sure was one fantastic sports grandmom—and this time around, with her grandson, I think she actually enjoyed it (when she was awake).

Fs and Us, Ps and Qs

=====

MY MOTHER WAS a stickler for manners. I'll never forget the first time she took me to a petting zoo. (I was thirty-seven; Mom was a procrastinator.) We saw a huge potbellied pig feasting on slop. She shook her head and said, "Look at that! He's got food on his whiskers, he's covered in mud, and he's chewing with his mouth open. It's like eating with your aunt Miriam."

My mother was born in 1933 and was raised in an era when simple manners meant a lot. She told me that her mother would never leave the house—not even to walk to the corner store—unless she was dressed "like a lady": that is, stockings, gloves, fur coat, hat. My mom said Grandma used to say, "It doesn't matter if no one on the street could see me; *I* could see me." On one hand, I think that's such an elegant and esteem-building way to behave. On the other hand, it seems like a huge pain in the ass just to get a loaf of bread. But it's easier for me to understand those times than it is for me to understand today, when many of the younger girls are getting tattooed from head to toe. I'm not judging; I like a little ink. I have a couple of small, discreetly placed tattoos myself. I just wonder how, sixty years from now, Nana is going to be able to explain to her ten-year-old grandson why she has a tramp stamp and a picture of a serpent coming out of a vagina on her chest. (I once heard a rumor that former secretary of state Al Haig had the Princeton tiger tattooed on his butt. Whether it was true or not, that image has never left me. I'm just grateful he didn't go to South Carolina; he'd have had a gamecock on his ass.)

When it came to etiquette, my mother was very old-fashioned and old school. She actually collected old Emily Post books to see how manners had changed through the years. Believe it or not, when she wasn't on the road, we frequently sat down together as a family and had a *formal* dinner. I'm talking French service with fingerbowls, and forks, knives, and spoons of every conceivable shape and size. I'm doing the light version of formal with Cooper, as I don't think his generation will need to know what a demitasse spoon is for. (Pity, because someday he's going to inherit four sets of them.)

My mom believed that men should be gentlemen, women should be ladies, and drag queens should make a friggin' decision so we know whether to treat them like ladies or gentlemen. Once, when I was in high school, I had a really big date with a football player. He was taking me out to dinner, and right before I left the house, my mother said, "Missy, I hope he behaves like a gentleman." I said, "What do you mean?" She said, "It's *his* job to bring the condoms and lube." I said, "Mom!" She said,

"I'm kidding. I hope he opens the door for you and pulls out your chair in the restaurant—and not while you're sitting in it."

She always said that chivalry wasn't dead, it was just hiding in Argentina like the old Nazis and it was her job to ferret it out.

My mother was especially focused on table manners. If she caught me eating with my fingers or chewing with my mouth open, she'd glare at me as though I'd run over the only child of a powerful world leader (or, more important, a powerful talent agent). When I was a little girl sitting at the dining room table, she'd say, "Is that how you're planning on eating when we're having dinner with the queen of England?" I bought that until I was eight years old, and then one night at dinner, I had an epiphany and said, "Wait a minute! You don't know the queen of England." Little did I know that twenty years later she would, but back then she was just being manipulative.

My mother felt that regardless of one's standing in life—or what one was eating—there was never an excuse for bad manners. She said that good manners, table or otherwise, start at home, and it makes no difference if you have money or not. The rules of civility are the same whether you were raised on the Kennedy compound or in Honey Boo Boo's trailer park. When my mother saw the movie *Deliverance,* she was stunned by the hillbilly rape scene in the woods. It wasn't the rough sex that horrified her; it was the fact that, the next day, not one of the hillbillies had the manners to send flowers, pick up a phone, or drop a simple thank-you card in the mail.

My parents felt it was never too early to teach a child proper manners. According to family legend, my first words as a baby were "Excuse me," spoken after I spat up on our nanny while she was burping me. As the story goes, Consuelo looked stunned, and to this day I'm not sure if it was because I had such good manners at such a young age or because she spoke no English and thought I was possessed by the devil and speaking in tongues (the day before she had taken a phone message from one of my mother's agents, so the devil was at the forefront of her mind).

I was taught that when I was introduced to my parents' friends, I was to address them as "Mr." or "Mrs."—unless the woman was single or the man was gay, in which case I was to address them both as "Miss." I remember once, when I was about ten or eleven years old, a new neighbor moved in across the street. She was very masculine, with close-cropped hair, man hands, Brooks Brothers suits, and wingtip shoes. I said, "Mom, what do I say to her? 'Hello, Miss Jones' or 'Nice to meet you, ma'am'?" My mother told me to crack my knuckles, give her a slap on the back, and say, "How's it hangin', Butch?" Apparently there was a whole different set of rules for lesbians she had not yet taught me.

My mother's show business career took us all over the world, and I learned that manners differ from country to country. For example, in Japan, burping at the end of a meal is considered a compliment. It means "Tell the chef the food was delicious." In this country, burping at the end of a meal is considered rude and means "Tell the chef to cook the fuckin' fish!"

I learned that in the Middle East, people are only allowed to eat with their right hands. My mother said that this was because half the people had had their left hands cut off for masturbating, shoplifting, or masturbating while shoplifting.

I was taught that in Korea during dinner it's considered a sign of respect to follow your elders' cues—that is, eat as they do. My mother told me that she and my father tried that once in Boca Raton, following the elders' cues, and it didn't work out too well. They had to eat dinner at 2:00 p.m. (soft food only), pass gas at the table, and then wander the parking lot for an hour looking for the car.

My parents raised me in a very traditional manner, which, in the world of show business, is an anomaly. For example, I did not know that it was considered the height of rudeness to turn down a second line of cocaine from your celebrity host's private stash. Imagine my embarrassment at my sixth-grade graduation party.

All joking aside, the rules of etiquette in Hollywood are vastly different from those in the real world. We've all heard stories of stars behaving badly—and I'm not talking about the overpaid-athlete-groping-the-flight-attendant bad, I'm talking the if-anyone-else-behaved-that-way-they'd-be-socially-ostracized-and-thrown-out-of-the-diner bad. For example, it's urban legend that during the filming of the *Pirates of the Caribbean* movies, in order to "get in touch with his character," Johnny Depp didn't brush his teeth or wash his hair. I'm surprised his costars didn't get in touch with the Health Department. Can you imagine that in any other business? Can you imagine if fat Lenny sitting in the cubicle next to yours at work did that? You'd be down at HR faster than you can say, "Lather. Rinse. Repeat."

Truth be told, my mother didn't care if you were nominated for an Oscar or worked for Oscar Mayer—she felt that if *everyone* were taught good or at least appropriate manners, we'd be living in a much more polite and civilized society.

Children Should Be . . .

You know that old axiom "Children should be seen and not heard"? My mom had her own version of it: "Pretty children should be seen and not heard, and homely children should not be seen or heard"—which meant our family gatherings were not filled with the raucous laughter of children but more like the sounds of a 60 Minutes interview, culminating with "Don't try to sell me that 'inner beauty' bullshit. Just call the electrolysis guy already."

The Gift of the Grab

When Crown Books told me they were planning on releasing this book on Mother's Day, I was a little uncomfortable. Perhaps that's because they made me the offer right after my mother's funeral—and I mean right after. I was walking down the aisle of Temple Emanu-El when a strange woman (who I later found out was to become my fabulous editor) pressed her card into my hand and made the international hand sign for "Call me!" I was so shocked that I almost waited until I was in the limo to pick up the phone. She said to me, as though she'd known me forever, "Melinda, I'm so sorry for your loss. How 'bout a Mother's Day book?" My first thought was "Are you kidding me?" But my second thought was "What would my mother have done?" So, naturally, my third thought was "Sell, baby, sell! This book would be a perfect Mother's Day gift." And I say "perfect" because not only is it a fun homage to my mom, *but also, now that she's gone, she can't return it to Amazon in exchange for Giuliana Rancic's new memoir (which my mother knew would refer to her in only the most glowing of terms).*

O N THE TOPIC of gifts, when I was a little girl my mother told me that there were three things everybody liked getting: (1) good news, (2) good gifts, and (3) good head. I knew exactly what she meant by the first two, and when she felt I was at an appropriate age (fifth grade), she explained the last one to me. (She also pointed out that if I were really good at number three, I'd never have to worry about number two. God, she was wise.)

My mother believed that gift giving was as important an ancient art as Kabuki, jujitsu, and leeching. She knew when to give a gift and when not to give a gift (shower, yes; shiva, no), and more important, when to give an actual gift versus a gift card. For example, at a wedding shower, it's okay to give a pregnant bride a gift card to Babies R Us, but it's not okay to give her a big T-shirt that reads, KNOCKED UP!

My mom always said that in the world of show business, gift giving is more than just a nice way of saying, "Hello," or "Thank you," or "I'm thinking of you." It's actually a way of saying, "I'm thinking of *me,* and hopefully this gift I'm giving *you* will somehow benefit *me* when you're casting your next film, TV show, or national commercial."

In the world of entertainment, gifting is especially important at the top, among the muckety-mucks and the boldface names. Studio and network heads always give their high-profile stars high-profile gifts, like a safari in Africa or a weekend in Bali, or twenty-eight days at Betty Ford. And the stars (at least the ones who've had tough-love therapists) usually give gifts to the important producers, who in turn sell them on eBay so they can use that money, instead of their own, to buy generic trinkets for their writers, runners, assistants, and secret girlfriends/boyfriends/dominatrices, and fetish models.

It's a challenge to buy gifts for celebrities or very rich people because (a) they already have everything, and (b) whatever you do buy for them, they can buy a better version of it for themselves, which means the gift has to be either very thoughtful or very specific.

For example, my mother was a good friend of Prince Charles's, which meant birthday shopping was a big dilemma. What do you buy for someone who owns Europe? A tea set? A toaster cozy? A garden gnome you found in *SkyMall*? Last year my mother came up with the perfect gift, something she knew Charles needed but didn't have: a fifty-dollar gift certificate from Forever 21. Even if the prince didn't use it himself, he could always tuck it away in his kilt to give spontaneously to one of Harry's "girlfriends" as a thank-you-for-parting gift. My mother was nothing if not practical.

She also had a sense of humor with regard to gift giving, especially with other comics. As many of you know, comedian Tracy Morgan was in a horrible car accident in June 2014 and was in the hospital for months. My mom liked Tracy, and since he wasn't able to receive visitors right away, she wanted to send him a gift that would put a smile on his face. So she sent him a bouquet of dead flowers, with a card that read, "These flowers would've been dead anyway by the time you get out of the hospital." She was told it not only put a smile on his face, but it actually made him laugh.

My mother believed that the *second* most important trait in a good gift was thoughtfulness; *expense* is the most important. When Richard Burton bought Elizabeth Taylor that gigantic Krupp diamond, do you think Liz said, "Oh, Dick, it's cute, but I was hoping for something more personal"?

According to her, a thoughtful gift is simply something you know the recipient *wants,* not *needs.* Let's say, for example, your uncle Lou *needs* a new kidney. That doesn't mean you have to give him one. Instead, you know he'll soon want a beautiful new fountain pen, so he can fill out his last will and testament.

The only time expense takes a backseat in the gift department is Christmas. My mother taught me that holiday gifts *don't* need to be expensive, just appropriate. Why spend a fortune at FAO Schwarz on a toy for your toddler when you know full well all the kid's going to do is try to eat the box? (As my mother would say, "Do your own Jodie Foster joke here.") You'd be much wiser to buy lots of toys at some discount store—the children won't notice the difference, and besides, you'll make all your money back in a class-action lawsuit when half the kids get sick from putting the cheap, Chinese-made game pieces in their mouths.

There is an exception to this rule, however. Each year, there seems to be one hot gift that every child needs, wants, or must have or *they'll die*. I'll never forget the Tickle Me Elmo incident. One year my mother was on the *Today* show and they were doing a segment about the hottest, impossible-to-get kids' toys of the year. Number one on the Hit Parade was the Tickle Me Elmo doll, which had sold out in twenty seconds. The only doll left in the New York metropolitan area was the one on display on the *Today* show set. My mother noticed Matt Lauer eyeing the doll covetously (probably for his own son, who is the same age as Cooper), so she made a beeline for it. According to a very unreliable witness (my mother), a pleasant interview quickly turned into a minor tussle and then into a UFC event. Matt and Mom both fell to the ground, wrestling each other to get at the doll. Suddenly my mother screamed, "My hip, my hip!" Matt, concerned that she really was hurt, regained his composure and bent down to help her up. With ninja-like reflexes, she grabbed the doll and ran. Long story short: Cooper got his Tickle Me Elmo, and Matt Lauer got a restraining order. Merry Christmas!

Another thing my mother taught me was to be mindful of people's religion when buying holiday gifts. Since Christians celebrate the birth of Christ, giving a Christian a Kardashian sex tape with Kim moaning, "Oh, Jesus," would not be a good idea. Similarly, because Muslims fast for the entire month of Ramadan, giving out baskets from the Carnegie Deli would be stupid. Jews celebrate Chanukah, so you can buy pretty much anything as long as you don't buy it retail.

The most important thing my mother said to me about holiday gift giving was "Never, ever buy a gift for a Buddhist. They are a kind and lovely and gentle people, but when you give a gift to a Buddhist, you have to *thank them* for taking it. The Buddhists may call this tradition, but honestly, Melissa, after spending six hours on line in Talbots buying a saffron muumuu for Cousin Sheila (who at sixty-five changed her name to Rama Hama), I call it bullshit."

My mother always felt that gift giving was more than just an art; it was also a means of communicating. It can be direct or indirect, subtle or, quite frankly, passive-aggressive. "Passive-aggressive?" you ask. Well, yes!

For example, let's say my mother sent you a set of very expensive scented candles. You might be thinking, "That fragrance will keep our house smelling fresh and inviting." What my mother was actually saying was, "I'm not setting foot in your place again until the odor of cat urine is gone." If my mother gave you a free session with a closet organizer, she was saying, "Your clothes have to go. You dress like an old, cheap whore." And if you received a gym membership, it meant one of two things: either (a) you were fat, and she was embarrassed to be seen with you, or (b) you needed to get laid, so she'd paid one of the gym's trainers to toss you a quickie because everyone's sick of you being such a bitch.

I still tear up thinking about how my mother was always looking out for others. She was such a giver. One year, for the holidays, she decided to give each member of our entire staff a free cosmetic procedure—within reason. (Don't forget: we're Jews, and to be honest, a couple of them needed way more than one procedure in order not to frighten children or to be seen in daylight.) I thought it was a horribly insulting gift to give people. My mother, though, thought she was giving the greatest gift *ever*. Turns out, she was right. They loved it! I haven't seen this much excitement since Dennis Rodman negotiated a peace treaty with the North Koreans.

So, gentle reader, what have we learned? Yes, sometimes people give you gifts because they love you. But other times they give you gifts because they'd love you more if you were thinner or prettier. And sometimes they give you gifts because someone gave the gifts to them and they didn't like them.

Which brings me to the old expression "Cleanliness is next to godliness." My mother disagreed. She felt regifting was.

First, let me be clear: there's nothing wrong with regifting. We've all received gifts that might not have been right for us but that we knew someone else would love. One year, I received an anonymous gift of a fur coat, which I found odd, because everyone who knows me knows I work for PETA and I don't wear fur. When I opened the box, my mother's eyes lit up. She said, "Oh my God! What are you going to do with that? You don't wear fur!" Before I could answer, she had the coat on—and lo and behold, it fit her beautifully, as if it had been made just for her! And, coincidence of coincidences, her name was stitched on the inside! I said, "Mom, did you buy this coat for me just so I'd regift it to you?" With a look of feigned shock bordering on disdain, she said, "Is that what you think? I am hurt and appalled that you would think that—and I've buried the cost so deep in the books you'll never be able to prove it."

You have to be careful when regifting; sometimes something can go terribly wrong. A famous TV personality who shall go nameless once gave a very, very expensive handbag to the senior producer of my mother's show. The producer was beyond thrilled, couldn't believe the gift she had received. She was on cloud nine—until she opened the bag up and looked inside. It was monogrammed: TO: [CELEBRITY WHO SHALL REMAIN NAMELESS SO I DON'T GET SUED], YOU'RE A TRUE STAR! FROM: YOUR FRIENDS AT [A NETWORK I WON'T MENTION BECAUSE I WOULD LIKE TO WORK FOR THEM SOMEDAY]. There's a lesson to be learned here: Treat regifting like a crime scene. Get rid of the evidence and bury the body. They should never know you were there.

My mother always said that when it came to celebrities, it was less important what you gave them than what you *didn't* give them. Here's a copy of last year's "What Not to Buy" list:

What *Not* to Buy Certain Celebrities
- Pair of shoes—Oscar Pistorius
- Book on tape—Marlee Matlin
- Chin-up bar—Sen. Mitch McConnell
- Mirror—Stevie Wonder
- DVD of *Yentl*—Mel Gibson
- Condoms—Mrs. Duggar (too late!)

- Salad Shooter—Rush Limbaugh
- Library card—Sarah Palin
- Books—Kanye West
- Skateboard—Stephen Hawking

Tips on Mother's Day Gifts

As both a daughter and a mother, I've learned a thing or two about giving good (read: appropriate) Mother's Day gifts. Here are a few suggestions that I hope will help you in the coming years:

• Never, ever, ever—I don't care what kind of pressure you're under, even if Dick Cheney's standing over you with his waterboarding kit—give your mother a vacuum, a Salad Shooter, or any household item that either requires her to work or can be construed as self-serving. For example, you say, "Happy Mother's Day, Mom! Here's your new washer-dryer." What she hears is "I'm thirty-five, not getting married anytime soon, and have no intention of doing my own laundry." I learned this the hard way. I once bought my mother a steam iron for Mother's Day. She thanked me by "allowing" me to sleep in the maid's room for a week.

• *Buy* something. Making a jewelry box out of Popsicle sticks is adorable—if you're seven. If you're old enough to be tried as an adult, you're old enough to put together a couple of bucks and hit a mall.

- Buy something that will make your mother feel good—a pair of fun, not-too-cheap earrings; a day of beauty at a local spa; a box of chocolates that says to her, "I Love You More Than My Birth Mom."

- Buy her something she'll always remember—like a framed photo of the two of you together, or an autographed copy of a book by her favorite author, or a gift certificate for a consultation with the world's best divorce lawyer.

- Don't buy a gift with an agenda. Last year my mother bought me three beautiful picture frames—complete with the photos of the lovely couples that had come with the frames. And in each photo, she'd cut out the woman's face and taped my face in its place. Forget thoughtfulness; think of the effort that went into making that gift so special! I'm surprised the card didn't read, "Happy Single Mother's Day!"

Readin', Ritin', and 'Rithmetic

You can never be overdressed or overeducated.

—OSCAR WILDE

UNLIKE MANY OF today's anti-intellectual, pandering politicians, my parents believed that education was the key to a better life. I think part of the reason is that both my father's and my mother's parents were immigrants. My father was one of the children of the Holocaust.* He was born in Germany in 1925 and lived there until the Nazis came to power and began their persecution of the Jews. His family fled to Denmark and then, when the Nazis marched in there, to Cape Town, South Africa. (South Africa proved to be a blessing for my father: it not only saved his life but also prepared him for

---

* I hate the expression "children of the Holocaust." It sounds like a new reality series on Bravo. Maybe it could have a sister series, *Real Housewives of Treblinka*.

life with my mother. It was his first experience with diamonds.)

After the war my dad was sent to school in the United Kingdom and eventually came to the United States. A few years later he brought his parents over, too. Because his family had to move constantly, and lost everything every time, my father often reminded me, "Education is the one thing they can't take away from you."

My mother's father was a Russian peasant who came to America and worked his way through medical school. Her mother was from a well-to-do Russian family that, like my father's parents, had to leave everything behind when they came here. So my mother and her sister, Barbara, learned the importance of education as a survival tool.

My aunt Barbara may have been a genius. Perhaps not on the level of internationally acclaimed genius Stephen Hawking or self-proclaimed genius Kanye West, but she was brilliant. She taught herself Russian and became fluent in it in one summer, just because she wanted to. She graduated from Columbia Law School at the age of twenty. There was seemingly nothing she didn't know, and most of it came naturally. And because she was so smart, during my mother's entire life, within the extended family my mom was known as "Barbara Molinsky's sister." True to her competitive nature, rather than allowing the fact that Barbara was "the smart one" to depress or upset her, my mother only became that much more motivated to work her ass off in school.

Which she did. Yet, from kindergarten and all the

way through Barnard, no matter how smart she was or how hard she worked, she never conquered arithmetic—a gift she generously passed on to me.

My mother (and I) could barely add and subtract. Her entire grasp of arithmetic can be summed up in one bit of advice she gave me when I was struggling in math class. She said, "Melissa, I can do tips and discounts, and figure out the number of gay men in an audience to make it a good show. That's all the math you'll ever need, unless you're planning on being an accountant."

Some Things Never Change

'VE OFTEN WONDERED if the personality traits we exhibit as children we continue to exhibit as adults. I offer up to you the closest I can get to scientific proof that this is so. Over the next few pages, I hereby present portions of my mother's report cards, grades one through four.

BROOKLYN ETHICAL CULTURE SCHOOL
49 AND 50 PROSPECT PARK WEST
BROOKLYN, NEW YORK
TELEPHONE SOUTH 8-4300

MRS. HENRY NEUMANN, DIRECTOR
MISS M. PAULINE RUTLEDGE, PRINCIPAL

Report on

JOAN MOLINSKY - GRADE ONE

From December 6, 1938 to April 3, 1939

(The original manuscript of this report has been read by Mrs. Neumann and by Miss Rutledge.)

Joan has made good progress in School this term. Her creative ability has found expression through art materials. She has a vivacious imagination. This is finding an outlet in original stories, poems and plays.

Joan has good habits of work and her attack on problems is better.

Her reading is good. Her writing has improved and shows the effort she has made.

Socially Joan has grown. She has learned to give and take., lead and follow, stand or fall in the effort to win leadership. She has also learned through actual experiences, that fair play is the only way. Joan possesses a fund of information concerning many fields of knowledge.

Her choice in activities is widening. Her concentration span is lengthening. She has grown more orderly in the care of her own belongings.

Joan's voice is still loud and she tries to gain attention this way. We are checking this habit as it occurs and seeing that the attention she wishes is not forthcoming when she is loud.

She has overcome many food dislikes this year. She rests well and she relaxes also.

In the yard she is much more active and joins more freely in all group games.

BOOKS READ

Playmates	-Pre Primer
Dick and Jane	-Pre Primer
The Little Book	-Pre Primer
Here and There	-Pre Primer
Friends for Every Day	-Primer
Friends	-Primer
Gates and Huber	-Primer

A. KASTNER

-:-

MRS. HENRY NEUMANN, Director
MISS M. PAULINE RUTLEDGE, Principal

Report on

JOAN MOLINSKY - GRADE II

From November 27, 1939 to April 15, 1940

(The original manuscript of this report has been read by Mrs. Neumann and by Miss Rutledge.)

Joan's academic work is very good. She is quieter and much less tense.

Joan is very cooperative and has learned to work independent of others in the group. She possesses original ideas as shown by her art work.

Joan has gained in self-confidence and appears happier. She does not act so fearful of making a mistake.

She leads in many group activities. Instead of dominating she has learned to cooperate and share her ideas with others. She seldom resorts to immature dramatic play.

Joan enters into all yard games, directed and free and enjoys playing with all members of the group. Recently she has learned to jump rope which has helped to give her additional security and to gain in self-confidence.

Joan still needs commendation for all of her good work. She reacts favorably when praised but is extremely sensitive to criticism.

Because she has been doing fine work she has been given "special art" in the art room.

Joan eats well and rests well.

Z. E. KRITZLER

-:-

REPORTS OF SPECIAL TEACHERS

MUSIC

Voice is pitched more accurately. We are doing individual work to improve tone quality and pitch. Joan is doing well in ear-training. Handles the beginning of reading and writing in staff notation without difficulty.

G. ROBERTS

DANCE

Joan continues to dance beautifully. She is very imaginative, very free, and has a marked sense of leadership.

R. HOFFMAN

Absent - 6   Tardy - 4

BROOKLYN ETHICAL CULTURE SCHOOL
49 AND 50 PROSPECT PARK WEST
BROOKLYN, NEW YORK
TELEPHONE SOUTH 8-4300

MRS. HENRY NEUMANN, DIRECTOR
Miss M. PAULINE RUTLEDGE, PRINCIPAL

Report on

JOAN MOLINSKY - GRADE THREE

From December 2, 1940 to May 5, 1941

(The original manuscript of this report has been read by Mrs. Neumann
and by Miss Rutledge.)

Joan continues to do good work in her academic subjects. She is
eager to do well and she has good work habits. We are giving her
special help in spelling. She worries when she cannot do a thing
well and we are encouraging her to do her best and know that is all
we expect of her.

Joan does interesting art work and should have good paints and
colored pencils at her disposal.

She is charming to her class-mates and does not seek one companion
as much as she did at the beginning of the year.

Joan is a pleasing member of the group.

L. LUCKEY

-:-

REPORTS OF SPECIAL TEACHERS

DANCING

Joan has made consistent progress. Her dancing is graceful,
rhythmic and imaginative. She is eager always to contribute either
alone or with the group.

R. HOFFMAN

SINGING

Her singing has improved in accuracy of pitch and quality. She
enjoys experimenting with instruments producing variations in sounds.
She is working well in ear training, rhythmic activity, and with
notation.

G. ROBERTS

SHOP

Joan has applied herself to her work in a satisfactory manner.
At times, excessive talking hampers the movement of her work.

E. PALEY

Absent - 13
Tardy - 8

BROOKLYN ETHICAL CULTURE SCHOOL
49 AND 50 PROSPECT PARK WEST
BROOKLYN, NEW YORK
TELEPHONE SOUTH 8-4300

MRS. HENRY NEUMANN, DIRECTOR
MISS M. PAULINE RUTLEDGE, PRINCIPAL

Report on

JOAN MOLINSKY – GRADE FOUR

From September 24, 1941 to December 5, 1941.

(The original manuscript of this report has been read by Mrs. Neumann and by Miss Rutledge.)

SOCIAL STUDIES

Joan has worked hard on our share of the festival. She did excellent work in making the properties. Her reading during social studies periods have given her a good fund of information.

ENGLISH AND LITERATURE

Her work in creative writing is very interesting. She used rich vocabulary as well as a lyric style. She reads widely and well and enjoys reading aloud to the group.

ARITHMETIC

Joan has made greatest growth in accuracy. We are working for neatness rather than speed.

PENMANSHIP

Her writing is much larger and freer. We are working for better letter form.

SPELLING

Joan is a good speller.

YARD

Joan is trying hard to participate in all yard games. She is less inclined to form small groups for immature play.

GENERAL

Joan is a happy, intelligent child. She is learning to be self-reliant and to gain recognition through accomplishment rather than through complaining. She is fast overcoming her tendency toward bribery in order to win friends.

R. BEFELER

–:–

REPORTS OF SPECIAL TEACHERS

MUSIC

Joan co-operates well and is a helpful member of the group. Her work shows greater self-confidence and is more demonstrative. She sings with a stronger voice and much improved sureness of pitch. She is using her creative ability in individual work and in handling the materials of music with the class.

G. ROBERTS

Brains vs. Boobs

Men don't want smart. They want gorgeous. No
man ever put his hand up a woman's dress looking
for a library card.

—JOAN RIVERS
on *The Tonight Show*

M Y MOTHER TRULY believed that men care more about
beauty than brains, and that a man would rather
spend twenty years with a stunning dunce than
twenty minutes with Eleanor Roosevelt. Yet she insisted that I go to college. For years I found that highly
insulting.

As a child I didn't go through the public school system; my parents sent me to private school. Not that they
had anything against public schools ("Missy, the only
thing wrong with public schools is the public"); they just
thought I'd thrive better in private schools. I personally
think they wasted their money. I grew up in Beverly Hills.

How bad could the public schools have been? I believe Beverly Hills has the only junior high school in the country that offers its students personal shoppers and cold storage for their furs. In our neck of the woods the only difference between the public and private schools was that in the private schools the drug dealers drove Bentleys, not low-riders.

Private schools are like colleges in that you have to be accepted by a board of admissions to get in. This is true today even for private nursery and pre-K schools. Parents have to "sell the school board" on their child, like they're prized pigs at auction. How many "extracurricular activities" could a three-year-old have? "Well, Headmaster Jones, in addition to knowing his ABCs and being able to identify most of the Muppets, in his free time little Billy likes to stack his juice boxes in size order and loves making symmetrical pancakes out of his BMs."

When I was in the elementary grades, or until the time I exceeded my parents' academic abilities, my mom and dad were *very* hands-on. They checked *every* bit of homework I had—or at least the assignments I told them I had. (I need to make amends here to my fourth-grade teacher: Sorry, Señora Diaz. I think I still owe you a few assignments. I'll try to get them to you before 2017.) My mother would help me with history, foreign languages, social studies, and humanities, and my father would help me with math. So as not to miss a moment of being involved, when my father was helping me with arithmetic my mother would sit on the floor next to us and take my Magic Markers and color in the worn spots on our Oriental rugs.

My parents made sure that all my assignments were not only factually accurate but that the grammar and punctuation also were correct. (This kind of attention to detail paid off last year when the piece I wrote for my mother's memorial service was considered by many to be a grammarian's wet dream. Mom, red pen in hand, would have been happy.)

My mother was very involved (i.e., competitive) when it came to class projects, but I think she came by that honestly.

In second grade my class had to do book reports. One little girl's father was a studio chief and had had the studio's art department mock up a storyboard for his daughter's book report presentation. This infuriated my mother because she is very artsy-craftsy and she hadn't cheated and helped me with my report. The only comfort was that the girl didn't get an A, although she did get an Oscar nomination for Best Art Direction.

Learning from that experience, my mother, over the past five or six years, tried to "get an edge" for Cooper in his class projects by trying to call in favors from her creative friends (like painter Robert Rauschenberg), but I watched her like a hawk, to make sure she didn't cheat to get him an A. I'd rather Cooper get a hard-earned B than a tainted A. (Yes, dear reader, I know what you're thinking: Tainted A *is* the private nickname of one of Hollywood's most famous actresses, but *no*, under the advice of counsel, I cannot tell you who it is.)

Unlike my mother, I am *not* artsy-craftsy, and I won't cheat, so Cooper's fifth-grade science class volcano was a little lopsided, and instead of erupting, it leaked. The good news was that none of the little cardboard people in Pompeii died in rivers of "lava"; they just got their shoes wet.

My mother's take on cheating was born of the best intentions—she wanted me to have the best education possible, which is why she and my father worked so hard to send me to the best schools. This was especially true after my elementary years, when I was heading into seventh grade. In Los Angeles, that meant the exclusive, academically demanding finishing school the Marlborough School for Girls. (Hard to guess from the name that it was WASPy, huh? The school mascot was a jar of mayonnaise. Ba-rum-bum.)

At the interview for Marlborough my parents said to the über-Anglo-Saxon head of admissions, "We know you have a quota system and our Melissa fills two of the boxes: showbiz and Jewish." And they still let me in. I was a human twofer!

I lasted at Marlborough until tenth grade, when the lockjawed, estrogen-filled WASPishness began overwhelming me. My parents felt I wasn't thriving as they'd hoped in the all-girls, cliquey school—where I was a year younger than my classmates because I'd skipped a grade—so they transferred me to the Buckley School, which was just as academically rigorous but offered things Marlborough didn't: less-mean girls, a kinder, gentler environment . . . and boys!

During my time at Buckley, shockingly, I spent a lot of time in detention (or the home version of detention: grounded) for things like ditching classes, violating the dress code, not doing my homework, and engaging in

"excessive fraternizing." With the exception of petty lar-
ceny, arson, and aggravated vandalism, I did it all—and I
was considered one of the *good* kids.

In hindsight, I see that nothing I ever did was all that
bad. I was just rebellious by nature, and I never understood why I was being forced to wear saddle shoes when
my topsiders, Vans, and Keds looked so much better with
the school uniform! (Ironic that my mother wound up on
Fashion Police in light of the fact that her own child went
to a school that made the students wear uniforms until
graduation. "Zere vill be no freedom of expression ven
it comes to fashion. You vill do as you are told and you
vill like it!" Little did I know that the "Catholic school
girl" look was actually a sexual fetish and that our school
was inadvertently prepping some of the girls for the items
they'd cherish later in life: g-strings, stilettos, sequined
thongs, and stripper poles.)

After Marlborough and Buckley came college. In the
Rosenberg-Rivers family, going to college wasn't a choice;
it was an understanding. (If I remember correctly, when
I was a senior in high school, I once said, in a passively
rebellious moment, "Mommy, I don't think I'm going to
go to college." She took a long pause and said, "Have
we met? You look familiar, but I'm sure I don't know
you.") Which college to go to wasn't much of a choice, either; my options were big Ivy League or small Ivy League
(there is no medium Ivy League). I could have had the IQ
of a houseplant and my parents still would have had me
filling out applications for Harvard, Yale, Brown, Dart-
mouth, and Penn. I believe my mother's exact words were
"Melissa, if you go west of the Mississippi, you pay."

For Cooper, going to college isn't a choice, either; it's an understanding. He is expected to live up to the same standards that were oh so gently forced upon me. I have already brainwashed my child as to what schools are acceptable: big Ivy or small Ivy. Although I have cut him some slack and let him pick Johns Hopkins and Duke as fallback schools, that's only because they have world-class lacrosse teams.

FYI, as I write this, Cooper is in eighth grade. But why procrastinate four years and wait until twelfth grade when I can start the nagging now?

The first interview for college my parents took me on was at buttoned-down, conservative, old-fashioned Williams. The Three Jew-migos drove up in a long, white stretch limo singing "We Are What We Are" at the top of our lungs. I went to Penn.*

_____

* From what I've been told, I had a very good time there.

Better Living Through Candy

LTHOUGH I WAS raised in Southern California, my parents were not your stereotypical kale-eating, granola-munching, meditation-loving West Coasters. I learned that all on my own. As an adult, I try to lead a healthy lifestyle—I eat right, I work out, and I take my meds on time. I'm in pretty good shape. This is because, when I was growing up, I took my mother's diet plan . . . and ignored it completely.

First off, as I mentioned before, my mother *never* cooked. Her signature dish was takeout. If she'd had a job as a prison chef, no one ever would have been executed. They'd never have received the last meal they were legally entitled to. Right up until the end of her life my mother believed that, in a pinch, ketchup, Altoids, and Milk Duds were a three-course meal.*

---

* I recently found out that, when travelling, my mother used to hide cash in empty Milk Duds boxes—they're the same size as paper money—so in case someone rifled her purse, they'd overlook it. This information came to light this past December, and I can't tell you the

That doesn't mean we didn't sit down to dinner together every night. We did. And my parents would start the meal by thanking God not only for the abundance of food, but also for the abundance of restaurants offering free delivery within thirty minutes. If my parents were going out for dinner, they'd set up a tray in their bedroom so I could eat while they were getting ready. This way we could still engage in family table talk—backbiting, celebrity gossip, and grilling me about my life as if it were the Spanish Inquisition. It was a simpler time.

To their credit, even though they were very busy and not even remotely involved in the culinary arts (defrosting was a challenge), my parents tried to do it right. They made sure I had at least the minimum daily requirement of vegetables, protein, and gummy bears. I was a terribly picky eater, but it wasn't my fault. It was hard to take my mother's nutritional advice seriously when she'd sit down at the dinner table and her plate was made up of M&M's, Fritos, and a glass of white wine.

My father had a different approach: he decided to forgo explaining the value of nutrition to me and simply pay me to eat. It's not that he didn't care about my health and well-being; he was just tired of arguing with me and realized that it was easier to trade cash for peace. (I like to think of myself back then as akin to a budding arms dealer or creating a blueprint for NAFTA.) After years of hounding and cajoling and bribing, they finally gave up when they walked into the kitchen one morning and found

---

chill that ran through my body, knowing how much cleaning we had done after she died.

me hunched over the sink having a breakfast of Pop Tarts and Diet Coke. When I got to college, I had an epiphany about nutrition. I realized that good-looking men weren't generally drawn to women who wolfed down Pop Tarts and Diet Coke hunched over the sink. So I started eating better and made sure that I was home alone, with the curtains drawn, before I ate microwave popcorn and Hot Pockets for dinner. And now, as a mother, I'm proud to say that Cooper does the same thing.

Boy Meets Girl (or Whatever)

WHEN IT CAME to my mother teaching/advising/cautioning/warning me about dating and romance, listening to her was like playing Truth or Dare with a pre-op transsexual: I never knew what I was going to get. On the one hand, my mother talked about love in an old-fashioned manner; on the other hand, she spoke like the whore of Babylon.

My mother felt that "courting" was a game I needed to know and know how to play. She fancied herself a modern-day courtesan in how she behaved and treated her men. To be fair, she did have two legitimate long-term relationships after my father's passing. I actually got to see her in her "courtesaning" mode, flirting with men she was interested in. The only thing I can say about that is it's one of those things that, once you see, you can't unsee, and it will haunt you for the rest of your life.

She always told me, "Dating is a game. When you're dating, trust me, they don't really love how you look when you don't have your makeup on, even though they say they do. They don't want to hear about your ailments and your worries. Men are basic: they want you to look pretty and be good in bed. Oh, and if you're smart and funny, that's nice—let your friends enjoy that side of your personality. No man ever wants to be reminded that women are truly superior. Yes, the truth makes them that insecure. You can be smarter than them or funnier than them, but not both."

One mantra she lived by was to "make sure the man *always* thinks he's the best and the smartest, and that every time you look at him, he thinks you're thinking, 'Honey, I need you.'" The fact that men are inherently stupid makes this not such a hard task to accomplish.

One of my mother's good friends was the wife of a famous billionaire financier—you can guess which one; I'm not telling. When my mother would have them over for dinner, her friend would sit at the table with her hand in her chin, hanging on her rich husband's every word. "Oh, sweetheart, that is so wise. You are such a sage." My mother said the only way she managed not to laugh or vomit was to look at the ring on her friend's finger and think, "Check out the ring on her finger; who's sage-ing whom?"

My mother treated her men the same way. She tried making them feel like they were the best things God had ever put on the planet, even better than Bergdorf or Saks.

She was coy, and was always about "making life better for her man." She instinctively knew what buttons to push to make a man feel good about himself, and would push them as needed. (Conversely, she knew which buttons to push to make me feel bad; of course she knew those buttons; she'd installed them.) She'd say things like "Oh, Lenny, I love the way your love handles drag on the floor; I don't have to vacuum," or "Milton, it really turns me on the way your hair plugs tickle my thighs." She may not have been honest in the boudoir, but she was smart. "Melissa, making a man's life better may take a little work and a little craftiness, but it will earn you large, shiny necklaces afterward." When I replied, "I can buy my own shiny necklaces," she said, "Of course you can; but why should you?"

My mother often gave me tips on dating. Some were actually good, and some were ridiculous. For example, she told me always to wear heels. They make your legs look better. (She even suggested to me that I play tennis in them.) "Even if he's just coming over to relax, answer the door in heels. You can always kick them off and curl your feet under you on the couch like Marilyn Monroe." Not a bad suggestion.

On the flip side, she also suggested that before a man came to the house to pick me up for a date, I should send flowers to myself so that when he walked in he'd be jealous and say, "Who sent you those beautiful flowers?" I don't know about anybody else, but not one man I dated ever noticed the flowers in my house. Not even the mortician I went out with once. (Don't ask. In bed he wanted to put pennies on my eyes and have me lie perfectly still.)*

My mother was from an era when men asked out women, and wined them and dined them in the hope of getting (a) a relationship, (b) a wife, or (c) a good roll in the hay. She used to tell me that when she was young, there were always one or two girls in her high school who were "fast" and who "put out," but most of them stayed virgins until they got married. "Things have changed, Missy. Now they only stay virgins until homeroom."

She believed that today's women have "fucked it up for themselves" because they give it up so quickly. On *Fashion Police* she hated seeing the young stars dressed like sluts because it sent a message that girls were available for the taking.

Her concern about teen sluttiness was genuine. My mom worried that a lot of today's youth would miss out on the wonderful rites of passage that she, and to some extent I, had. She used to talk about the innocent experiences of flirting, and passing notes in class, and holding hands. As forward-thinking and trend-conscious as she was, she was still old-fashioned in certain ways. She didn't like everything about modern technology. "Melissa, in my day a boy asked you out, bought you flowers, and had you home at a reasonable hour. In high school we had boyfriends and girlfriends, not baby daddies and baby mamas. I hear about all these college kids sexting pictures of their junk. It's not right. If I want to see a young penis, I'll take a shower with Chaz Bono."

---

* More of my mother's dating tips on the next page!

DATING TIPS MY MOTHER GAVE ME

- Take breath mints with you. No man, not even one with BO and a sinus condition, wants to kiss a girl who has the breath of death.

- Always have lipstick, powder, and a mirror in your purse. It takes five minutes to freshen up and look good, but it only takes five seconds with lipstick on your teeth to ruin a relationship.

- Never pick up the check. "You have the vagina, he has the wallet. He pays."

- Let him open the door for you. If he doesn't, and leaves you standing in the street, turn around, get in a cab, and go home. If he leaves you in the street, he'll leave you for another woman.

- Never give it up on the first date, because once you do, you give away your power. And once you give it up, you'd better make sure you're so good at it that it's like an addiction. (She would actually send me articles on how to be good in bed and how to give good blow jobs. I'm surprised she didn't try to hire me a tutor.)

- Never carry condoms. Those are his responsibility. "Women who carry condoms don't look like Girl Scouts who are always prepared; they look like prostitutes who are always at the free clinic."

- Make sure he's straight. Gay men make great BFFs but lousy boyfriends. Any man who mentions Bette Midler more than once a year, or who gets giddy when he realizes that you two look good in the same colors, is probably not a good dating choice. ("Hey, honey, check this out: we're both autumns!")

- Google him before you do him. No sane woman wants to have toe-curling, I've-already-fallen-in-love-with-you sex with a man only to find out later that he's got wives and families in nine different states or is wanted by the FBI, CIA, Interpol, and ISIS.

My mother read somewhere that you will have five great loves in your life, so if one of them breaks up with you, it's not a great loss. Then she added, "Unless it's breakup number five, and then you're fucked and you face a future of lesbianism, religion, or D batteries."

Everybody's Talking...
About Everybody Else

W HEN MY MOTHER wasn't quoting the world's greatest philosophers, writers, doctors, and scientists, she'd be quoting the only people she held in even higher esteem: gossip columnists. She'd been a close friend of the *New York Post*'s Cindy Adams since the day they first met, in 1847. She had a great relationship with Liz Smith, and was friends with everybody at TMZ, Radar Online, Perez Hilton, etc.*

---

* The irony in my mother's love of gossip columnists is the fact that she rarely, if ever, read things written about her. She had this steadfast rule that if a reporter or a blogger or some other random media type said or wrote something nasty about her, unless it was absolutely imperative, no one was allowed to tell her about it. "Melissa, I don't need to hear strangers say terrible things about me; that's why I have family." I get it. While I don't believe that ignorance is bliss (I'm not in Congress, after all), I also don't believe in getting my feelings hurt unnecessarily—which means even though I hope you really enjoy this book, if you don't, my feelings won't be hurt, because I won't know about it. I have this steadfast rule . . .

My mother hated the term *gossip columnist*. She found it pejorative, much like the terms *Soviet dissident* and *radical feminist*. (She much preferred *pissy Russki* and *single woman*.) She believed that if the public had an interest in the subject matter, then it wasn't gossip; it was news.

"Melissa, I don't think of celebrity reporting as mindless gossip. I think of it as a healthy exchange of information about people who influence our thinking and effect change in the world; people who make our lives fuller and richer; people like Oprah Winfrey and Steven Spielberg and two-thirds of One Direction."

One of her favorite columnists of all time was Maxine Mesinger of the *Houston Chronicle*. Maxine was the Walter Winchell of the West; she had enough clout to help make or break a young career. My mother once said, "Maxine Mesinger can give you Texas." She and my mother became fast friends from the moment they met, and not just because Maxine had power (although, God knows, it didn't hurt). She was a southern belle, smart as a whip, and hilariously funny. My mother spoke about Maxine the way lepers spoke about Jesus, in terms so glowing I imagined Maxine kicking off her heels and walking on water. (Not that there's any water in Houston—the place is completely landlocked and a thousand degrees. Last time I was there, the only water I saw were the puddles of sweat falling off me as I swatted away flies and mosquitoes.) My mother cited Maxine often, but one quote—having nothing to do with celebrity—stands out above all others. Shortly after I'd graduated from college and was getting ready to embark on my professional life, my mom sat me down and, with a tear in her eye, said, "Honey, always remember what the most important thing your auntie Maxine said: 'Sweetheart, pussy pulls freight trains.' " There's some maternal advice for you.*

---

* Writing this paragraph reminds me of the time my elementary school showed the movie *The Ten Commandments* on one of our monthly film nights. I liked the movie but two things stuck out. 1) Moses was Jewish; why was Charlton Heston cast to play him? Was Paul Newman unavailable? Was Tony Curtis doing dinner theater in Phoenix? 2) I didn't understand commandment number ten, "You shall not covet your neighbor's house; you shall not covet your neighbor's wife, nor his male servant, nor his female servant, nor his ox, nor his donkey, nor anything that is your neighbor's." When I got home from school, I asked my mother what that meant, and she said, "It means don't fuck your neighbor's wife and steal their sheep"—or maybe she said, "Don't fuck their sheep and steal their wife"; it's been a while so I'm paraphrasing, but I do know that I said, "Mr. and Mrs. Fleckman don't have a sheep."

My mother may have had few boundaries and lived a very public life, but she knew where to draw the line. You never saw a photo of her in a tabloid getting freaky wit' her baby daddy.

She never understood why actors and celebrities were always caught "canoodling" in some restaurant. (FYI, canoodling is a tabloid word meaning "making out," and is not to be confused with cornholing, which is a southern word meaning "be nice to your cousins.")

"Missy, I don't understand why celebrities think it's okay to make out in restaurants and theaters. It's a public place. Who else behaves like this? Did you ever see a chiropractor sucking his wife's toes in a Taco Bell? I think not."

"I Want to Live Forever ..."

M Y MOTHER HATED the kids on the network television show *Fame*,* which was based on (and which featured some of the kids from) the big hit movie *Fame*. (Okay, she didn't really hate them; she just couldn't figure out why they were all thirty-five years old and still in high school. It was her belief that if you were in high school at thirty-five you must've been one of two things: you were either a Cuban playing baseball with a fake birth certificate or you were left back seventeen times, in which case you shouldn't be in high school; you should be in *The Guinness Book of World Records* as "the world's stupidest person." That belief came honestly. She often told me stories about a guy she knew in high school named Marvin Lee. Marvin was a star football player who spent a really, really long time in high school. And by "really, really long time," I mean *every* day was father-son day

---

* For those of you too young to remember the movie or television show *Fame*, I'm going to make it easy for you: it's *Glee* with a less attractive student body.

at school, because Marvin had been there so long that he and his son were in the same grade. My mother put it very succinctly when she said, "Melissa, Marvin Lee was in high school for so many years they eventually just made him security.")

While my mom may not have liked the kids on *Fame,* she loved fame and she loved being famous. She was once asked on *The View,* "What's the downside of being famous?" She said, "None. There is no downside to being famous. It's all great!"

As far back as I can remember, my mother was always gracious to her fans. She signed every autograph and took every photo fans asked for. When I was about thirteen, my mother had two weekend performances at a theater in Chicago. One Saturday afternoon we decided to go shopping on Michigan Avenue. Every twenty feet, fans approached my mother, and she stopped and talked to every single one of them. After about an hour of this, we still hadn't gotten close to a store. My father leaned over and whispered in my ear, "I think we ought to make a movie about your mother walking down the street. We'll call it *Around the Block in Eighty Days.*"

There were a lot of benefits to growing up with a famous parent, and not just the financial ones. Our family rarely, if ever, had to wait on lines to get into a movie or a play or a concert. At restaurants, we always got reservations and always got the best tables and the best food. We never had to go through security lines at airports—the airline provides greeters who meet you at the curb and take you directly to security. As an aside, just because you went to the front of the line didn't mean the TSA gave you special treatment. With all the jewelry my mother wore and all the shit she had crammed in her carry-on (see the chapter "Fly Me to the Moan"), by the time she took everything off and put it in individual plastic bins, I guarantee at least 30 percent of the people behind her had missed their flights.

My mother couldn't stand celebrities who complained about the "burden" of fame. She'd say, "I hate the whiners who complain, 'I can't go anywhere in public. I have no privacy, people don't leave me alone, blah blah blah.'" Her answer to this was always the same: "If you need some privacy, stay inside the twenty-million-dollar gated mansion that fame has afforded you. Or go work in a morgue. No one will bother you. So, shut up!"

I'll never forget one night when my godfather, the actor Roddy McDowall, was at my parents' house for dinner. He was telling us a story about a conversation he had just had with Frank Sinatra. Frank was complaining that he couldn't go anywhere in public without being recognized and hounded. I guess my Uncle Roddy had had enough of Frank's "whining" and he turned and said to him, "There's a very simple solution. Take off your toupee, put on a pair of glasses, and ditch the bodyguard. You'll look just like any other older Italian man walking down the street."

My mother believed that if you were a star, once you got out in public, you were public property. This didn't mean she thought it was okay for paparazzi to harass stars' children on their way to school, or have helicopters fly over someone's house to get a picture. In fact, the only time she refused photos was for the first month after my dad died. I was a teenager, and she wanted to protect me as best she could. She would shake hands, but no pictures. She felt children were off-limits (unless they were in the biz as well). As she got older she became as protective of Cooper as she was of me when I was a child. "Melissa, I signed up to be famous. Cooper didn't. When he's an adult, if he wants to be famous—and I don't know why he wouldn't—*then* the paparazzi can take pictures of him when he's coming out of airports or restaurants or rehab. But not until then!"

"Realize how lucky you are. Fame is not a burden."

Just Say "Yes"

Melissa, when it comes to work, pretend you're a hooker during Fleet Week: Say "Yes" to Everything.

—JOAN RIVERS

MY MOTHER ONCE told me, "No one ever died from working too hard." I told her, "I beg to differ. The average life span of cavemen was seventeen years. If they had stopped hauling rocks and felling dinosaurs for a couple of minutes and taken a little R&R, or maybe a couple of random "me weekends," who knows, maybe they would have lived to be twenty." She thought about it and said, "Point taken, but maybe all they needed was some good live-in help."

When I was growing up I *always* had to have a job. My parents worked, my grandparents worked, I worked. I think we must have been the long-lost Jewish relatives of René Descartes, because our family motto was "We work, therefore we are." It didn't matter whether we had money. I was taught responsibility at an early age. If I concentrate really hard, I can go all the way back to being an infant in a crib and seeing my mother leaning over me and saying, "Burp and diaper yourself, Melissa. No one likes lazy." From the time I could carry a dish without breaking it, it was my job to clear the table, even though we had professional help—and clear it properly, the way the staff in a five-star restaurant would, *not* the way Mrs. Ginsberg next door did: throwing Melmac plates in a bus tray and leaving them in the sink until morning. Clearing a table properly meant that after the main course, all the bread-and-butter plates and salt and pepper shakers came off the table immediately, assuming you were eating in the American style—that is, salad first. (If you're going Continental—which I'm sure many of you do—then it's a different set of rules altogether, but rest assured, I knew those, too.)

I had to do the standard chores most kids had to do: I had to make my bed, help with laundry, walk the dog, etc., although my mother's approach to get me to perform these tasks was unique. The day before my tenth birthday party, due to either excitement or sloth, I left my room a disaster. Even though my parents had asked me for days to clean it up, it was a total mess. My mother opened the door and stood there, silently, with a look of disgust on her face. She didn't yell at me or punish me or pull a Joan Crawford and make me scrub the floor with a toothbrush. She just stood there, for what seemed like forever, and then very quietly said, "Do you know who leaves their clothes on the floor? The homeless, that's who. If you'd like to live in a refrigerator box around the corner, let me know; I can arrange it. You know whom I'm friends with? You've heard of Sears and Roebuck? Roebuck."

I always had summer jobs. One summer I worked on the beach crew of the Sand and Sea Club in Santa Monica, setting up chairs and umbrellas. There was no tipping allowed, but the old ladies would sneak us quarters. What they thought a quarter would buy, God only knows (it was 1989, not 1889), but by the end of the summer, I'd saved enough money to buy my own refrigerator box. Heh! That'll show her.

Another summer, I worked at a retail store, Camp Beverly Hills, working on the floor as a "sales assistant," which meant doing whatever task, no matter how menial, I was asked to do. The takeaway from that job, other than the minimum-wage paycheck and the realization that I might not be a "people person," was that I finally understood my mother's horror at the sight of my room on the day before my tenth birthday. Customers are pigs. To this day, I cannot leave a messy fitting room when I'm shopping, due to my "summer in retail."

When I was a teenager and competing in equestrian events, if I wanted to ride, I had to help out working in the barn—cleaning tack, washing horses, and rolling bandages. Other than walking behind the horses with a shovel and a bucket, I did everything, and I did it happily. Happily because, if I grumbled or had a sour look on my face, my mother would've made sure I *was* walking behind the horses with a shovel and a bucket. All the other riders, my peer group, just came and went, but I had to clean before I was allowed to join them. A small portion would be taken off my parents' bill every month in exchange for my services. My parents were trying to teach me about responsibility and the value of work. In spite of my grumbling teenage resistance to their plan, in hindsight, I see that they were right. If you really want something, you'd better be prepared to work hard for it, and the work ethic that they taught me has served me well my entire life. Of course, I didn't appreciate that until I was forty-one. I don't think twenty years is too long to hold on to resentment, do you?

Speedy Gonzalez

ONE OF THE most basic rules of successful parenting is that when dealing with children, both parents have to be on the same page. One of the most basic rules of teenagedom is to divide and conquer. As I've mentioned before, my parents felt I was a study in recessive genetics. However, the one place I clearly did not fall into the recessive department was in my ability to assess a situation in order to achieve my desired goal. I normally had a high batting average when it came to this kind of manipulation, but the following incident is an example of a full swing and miss. It was such a swing and miss that you'd have thought I played for the Mets.

When I was sixteen I got a speeding ticket while driving. (Shocker! A teenager speeding! How unusual!) Mind you, I wasn't doing a hundred miles per hour in a school zone, or whizzing through a hospital parking lot knocking patients out of wheelchairs, or crashing through a farmers' market, flattening vegetarians who were shopping for fresh, crisp lettuce. I was on my way home from school and was simply testing the cornering ability of my car.

Since I was already in trouble with my mother for something or other—this was the normal state of affairs during my teenage years; I spent more time in trouble with her than not, and had actually found a certain comfort zone in the relentless groundings, icy stares, and stony silences—I immediately went to my *father* and told him I'd gotten the ticket. I knew that my father, having a bit of a lead foot himself, would be significantly more understanding than Driving Miss Crazy. I begged him not to tell my mother—and I mean *begged,* like a hostage on *Criminal Minds* fighting to be unchained from the radiator in the basement before the maniac sets off the bomb's timer. Being in trouble with the police and the DMV was one thing, but having my name on my mother's shit list—not in pencil, in ink—was a whole 'nother kind of trouble.

My father, the dear, sweet, easily-manipulated-by-his-daughter's-tears man that he was, swore he wouldn't say anything and promised he would go to juvenile traffic court with me. And most important, he would never tell my mother. All was good in Melissaland.

But the day before my scheduled court appearance, my father found out that he couldn't go with me at the scheduled time, as he had a pressing business matter to attend to. So he wrote a letter to the court stipulating that his assistant, Dorothy, was his legal proxy and that she had the authority to appear with me in court on his behalf. Sounds good, right?

Wrong.

The next morning, during my mother's normal daily snooping sweep of the house, she found the note on my father's desk. She was apoplectic. Not only was she furious at me for getting the speeding ticket, but she was livid with my father for not only not telling her about it, but also knowingly and willingly engaging in a cover-up. For a man whose reading habits rarely strayed from history, she was shocked that my father had learned nothing from Watergate. She tore the note up and announced that *she* would be going to court with me.

Great.

Can I just say that the drive from our house to the courthouse was more awkward and uncomfortable than a homophobic congressman trying to explain to his wife why he was caught loitering in a men's room?

When we walked into court, all the other scofflaws and their families obviously recognized my mother, but she had a look on her face like Mel Gibson looking at his family tree and realizing that one of his relatives was Jewish. Not only did no one approach her for an autograph or photo, but they gave us a *Queen Mary*–size berth.

When my case came up on the docket and my name was called, my mother stopped being Joan Rivers or Joan Rosenberg and turned into Hangin' Judge Joan. The judge read the complaint against me and said, "How do you plead?" Before I could say, "Guilty," "Not guilty," or "Guilty with explanation," my mother cut me off and barked, "She's one hundred percent guilty and needs to go to traffic school!" The judge concurred, and that was that.

On our silent ride home, she managed to run a Stop sign, make an illegal U-turn, and clip a curb while making a left. I recognized the irony of this but thought better of saying anything. I also thought she would have been a great judge at the Salem Witch Trials.

Around six o'clock that evening the ice between my mother and me began to thaw. Shockingly, this coincided with my father's car coming up the driveway. Thanks, Dad! I owe you one.

A House Divided

MY PARENTS HANDLED problems differently, as you'll see in these two notes I found while researching this book. They were written to me by my father and mother, in response to some horrible teenage behavior I must have displayed. (I don't remember what the incident was—there were so many.) My mother liked to deal with problems head-on; my father liked to deal with them with his head in the sand.

Dear Melissa —

Sometimes it is very hard to grow up — to learn to be independant and to become totally your own self —

Today was one of those days. You are finding out about the thin line that divides friendship and respect. It is very difficult to know sometimes when you have gone "too far" — but keep trying. For 14 years of age, both Daddy & I are amazed at your maturity, your self confidence and in most cases, your adult understanding of situations.

You're allowed a few slips. Today was one of them.

I love and adore you.

Mommy —

P.S. Your still grounded, you little rat.

Edgar Rosenberg

My Darling Melissa,
   I apologise for being
so brusque with you this
morning – but I did'nt know
that you had worked things
out with Mummy the night
before – so I apologise again
for questioning you. I have
been a beat behind as
to what is going on and
my brains are a bit scrambled
from fatigue.
   I love you so
so much and I trust you
totally
         With all my love
            Daddy

"Your father didn't care if I went to bed mad. He cared if I went to Bergdorf mad."

Mirror, Mirror

M Y MOTHER WAS a looksist, which is an actual word, not a term I made up, the way many notable writers do. For example, Edgar Allan Poe coined the word *tintinnabulation,* for his classic poem "The Bells"; John Milton came up with *pandemonium* for *Paradise Lost;* and the legendary auteur Justin Bieber coined the universal catchword *belieber.* (I know Anne Frank would have been a belieber!) According to Wiktionary, a *looksist* is "someone who forms prejudices based on a person's physical appearance." My mother did that, in spades, and unabashedly.

As everyone reading this must know, appearances mattered to my mother, *a lot,* even more than money, if you can believe it. I'll never forget the time we were sitting in a synagogue in New Jersey (Temple B'nai Something or Other), for the funeral of some distant uncle, and the rabbi was droning on and on and on. My mother was dozing off, her eyes half open, sitting straight up. (She could actually do this; I have pictures to prove it—and no, I'm not putting them in the book. I'm going to meet up with her again someday, and all that Pavlovian training about "what happens in Malibu stays in Malibu" has paid off.) After being nudged awake for the third time, she leaned over and whispered to me, "This asshole is killing me. Let's play a game of 'Marry, Fuck, or Kill?' Your three choices are George Clooney, Howard Hughes, and Joey Buttafuoco. Go!" I thought about it, and waited to make sure the rabbi wasn't looking at us during the Kaddish, and said, "I'd marry George Clooney, I'd kill Joey Buttafuoco, and I'd fuck Howard Hughes." She looked horrified. She said, "You'd fuck Howard Hughes?! Are you crazy? He's filthy!" I said, "Yeah; filthy rich! Think about that." She said, "I did; that's why you don't fuck him, you marry him. Then you don't *have* to fuck him; his girlfriends will; and when he dies, you get the money *and* you didn't have to boil your lips or bathe in Purell." Even in mourning, she shared her wisdom.

I think the cause of her obsession with appearances was that for most of her life she was never happy with how she looked, which fed into her sense of being "less than." Growing up, her sister was the pretty one *and* the smart one; my mother felt second best. All her early self-deprecating material came from an honest place. And sadly, I inherited that gene—and what she believed was her original nose. Thanks, Mom. Appreciate it!

This is reflected in some of her early stand-up material. If you Google some of her first appearances on *The Ed Sullivan Show* or *The Tonight Show*, you'll see that in a lot of her jokes she was putting herself down, and most of those jokes were about her looks. "On my wedding night,

Edgar said, 'Why don't you undo your buttons?' I said, 'I'm already naked!'" Great joke, but my mother was not flat-chested. Yet, based on her self-perception as the ugly duckling, that joke was born of truth. (Interestingly enough, later in her career, while she was still poking fun at herself, she also started taking on celebrities and telling the truth about them. One of the reasons she got away with it was because she told the truth about herself first. After she died, a lot of people in the media mentioned that one of the reasons she was beloved was because she "said the things everyone else was really thinking.")

Last summer, on a day off between tapings of *Fashion Police* and *In Bed With Joan,* my mother and I were having lunch in Santa Monica with Joe F., one of her overly spiritually evolved AA friends. In the middle of an intense conversation about which were the correct shoes to wear with burkas, Joe F. blurted out, for no apparent reason, "What other people think of me is none of my business." Chalking up his off-point non sequitur to too much twelve-step work, my mother quietly smiled and replied, "Yes, it is! Especially if I'm one of those people." Two glasses of wine later, she was still rambling on. "Joe, . . . can I call you F? F, you . . . are an idiot. If you're on death row, headin' down the hall to Ole' Sparky, you think what the governor thinks of you doesn't matter? I rest my case." Sadly, after this lunch, Joe F. had only "one day back." Apparently she not only rested her case, but she also made Joe reconsider his sobriety and the point of living.

As a person who had changed her own physical appearance more than three hundred forty-eight times, my mother believed she had a moral and civic obligation to help make the rest of the world a prettier place. This was not some new, self-righteous, post–plastic surgery philosophy; she'd always felt this way. Way back in her early stand-up career in the 1960s, she had a joke that went "Lady Byrd Johnson wants to beautify America. She ought to start by keeping her daughters inside the house."

My mother understood DNA. She didn't blame the genetically homely. She knew that if a girl had her father's snout and her mother's tail, it wasn't her fault. But that didn't mean she shouldn't make an effort. My mother didn't like people who didn't try to do the best with what they had. This is one of the reasons she had little patience for movie stars who had the money and the means to look like movie stars, but didn't.

I'm not talking about great leading ladies and leading men* like Meryl Streep or Helen Mirren or Denzel Washington (who are perfectly fine looking). I'm talking about Cary Grant and Rita Hayworth and Vivien Leigh et al. They were all good actors, but according to my mother, audiences didn't go to see their movies because they were masters of the Stanislavski method or the Meisner technique; they went because they were gorgeous. One night we were having a girls' dinner at my house,† and over

---

* A "leading man" or "leading lady" is usually granted that moniker because of their unique beauty and their ability to light up a screen—and pack a house. "Character actor" means not pretty enough to carry a movie but so talented that you don't realize that the pretty one can't act. (This also applies to singers, like Mariah, one of the great voices of all time. If you ever watch her dancers, you'll notice they always dance around her, so you don't notice she can't do more than shuffle back and forth and from side to side.)

† A couple of times a year, my mother and I would host a "girls' dinner," attended by only our closest female friends and a handful of

dessert my mother asked, "Ladies, show of hands. Would you rather spend twenty bucks to see Ian McKellen in *Richard III* or Channing Tatum in a Speedo?" It was unanimous.

She never understood today's generation of celebrities who say, "I just want to look like myself." She'd say, "Really? What if myself is hideous? If you're George Clooney or Angelina Jolie, then by all means, 'look like yourself,' but if you're anyone else, take a shower, put on some blush, and demand backlighting, even if you're going to the supermarket!"

I always wondered what it would be like to be Heidi Klum or Angelina Jolie and look in the mirror and see that kind of beauty reflected back at you. Do they see what we see? Does Heidi see a Teutonic goddess whose smile lights up a room? Does Angelina see the thousands of teenage boys happily going blind because of her? In his book *Stories I Only Tell My Friends,* Rob Lowe acknowledges that he knew he was good looking, but then he talked about how tough it was being pretty. Fuck that. I'll take pretty over personality any day.

Clearly my mother felt the same way.

When Cooper was younger, the running joke was that he called my mother "Nana New Face," because every time he saw her, she had a new face. She changed noses the way Taylor Swift changes boyfriends—every few weeks. Ba-rum-bum.

Actually, she didn't have as much work done as peo-

---

fabulous gay men. (They bring much better gifts than straight women or lesbians.)

ple think she had. On a scale of one to Michael Jackson, she was a six. For example, she didn't change her race or gender, just her chin and eyes. She went from being a young, attractive woman with low self-esteem to an old, attractive woman with better self-esteem. Michael Jackson went from being a small black man to a thin white woman (who eerily looked like a cross between Elizabeth Taylor and Brooke Shields, with just a touch of Diana Ross).

My mother took this beauty thing very seriously. In fact, she spent a lot of time doing research to support her case. "Melissa, go back to the Bible. You've seen the pictures of Adam and Eve. Were they dogs? No. They were very attractive—and surprisingly pale considering how much time they spent in the sun. Granted, those pictures were an artist's rendering, but let me tell you, that artist was a maestro with a grease pencil."*

When I was in eleventh grade we went on a family vacation to Italy and France. When we were in Paris my mother spent the first five days pointing out all the places where French people had been rude to her. Then we hit the museums. When we were in Florence, Italy, we saw Michelangelo's statue of David. I told my mother how handsome he was. My mother replied, "You know that's not his original nose." And then she said, "You're right, Missy, he is handsome. People like beauty. But look— he's not Jewish. Ucch." (FYI, she had something to say about all of the great works. "Mona Lisa didn't smile

---

* He was the world's first police sketch artist. If not for him, they never would have caught Cain for killing Abel.

because she had rotten teeth. They had no fluoridation in her town, plus she smoked like a chimney. Venus de Milo? Played the handicapped card for all it was worth. Parked anywhere she wanted. I give her credit; she saved a fortune on gloves.")

The great thing about my mother was that, toward the end of her life, I think she had gotten to a place where she knew she looked good. Her whole thing was "Life is hard enough; you might as well do what you need to do to make yourself feel better." I find comfort in knowing that for all the plastic surgery jokes she made about herself—and that were made by others at her expense—she did what she needed to do to feel better. On her eightieth birthday she said to me, "You know what? For eighty, I don't look so bad." Better late than never, the swan appeared.

Bogey & Bacall

I N HOLLYWOOD, MORE so than anywhere else in the country, looks matter. (If you think I'm kidding, when is the last time you heard a movie star say, "You have *got* to go to my Botox guy. He's in Bismarck, South Dakota"?) There are more original ideas in Hollywood than faces, and there are almost zero original ideas in this city. Don't believe me? Check out the top five shows on television: *NCIS, NCIS Los Angeles, NCIS New Orleans, NCIS Cleveland, NCIS Levittown,* and *NCIS in a Pittsburgh Suburb.* (I hear there's another spinoff coming: *NCIS Corpus Christi.* Three Jewish cops spend twenty-six episodes trying to find a good corned beef and pastrami on rye. Spoiler alert! They fail.)

The media refer to Hollywood stars as the beautiful people, and that's because most of them are. Movie stars are movie stars for a reason, and talent isn't always the main one. Some of them are just so damned good-looking that people will pay to see them. Name one other profession, other than prostitution, where looks trump all other skills? (In the past, *actress* was often used as a euphemism for *prostitute,* and knowing what women in the entertainment business have to do these days to get equal pay, it's not that far from the truth.) Seriously, do you really care what your dermatologist looks like? Unless his face looks like a dartboard, you're not paying him for his killer eyes; you're paying him for what he can do with the wrinkles around *your* eyes.

My mom believed that as she got older, in order to stay in front of the TV cameras, she couldn't look like she was going to crack the lens. She also believed that it was more important for women to look good in Hollywood than for men. She was a realist, one who had an understanding of show business and its history. Truth be told, she was wildly irritated that we lived in a world where we needed a feminist movement. I think that's because when my mother started out in comedy, it never dawned on her that she might be at a disadvantage because she was a woman. It was so obvious to her that she just had to be funnier than everyone else, regardless of gender. It didn't matter what they had in their pants; it mattered what they had in their acts. When I told her that in one of my college textbooks she was referred to as a feminist icon, she said, "Oh, don't be silly, Melissa. Feminists are just lesbians who can't play golf." I said, "Is Gloria Steinem a lesbian?" She said, "I don't know, I've never slept with her. But I do know she hasn't broken par since 1987." (When I asked her if she ever burned her bra, she replied, "No; my boobs were never perky enough to go braless.")

My mother used to cite famous couples to prove her

point that looks were more important for women than for men.

She sat me down one day over a chicken salad and Botox lunch, to make sure I knew what she was talking about. She had drawn up a flow chart to get her point across. (At one point early in my life, my parents were told I was a visual learner, whatever that means.) Bogey and Bacall were her number one case study. "Lauren Bacall was a knockout. Lauren was tall, sexy, and had a smoky voice and killer eyes. Humphrey Bogart was short and swarthy, and he had buckteeth, a lisp, and he dragged a leg. Yet *he* was the bigger star and the sex symbol." Next up on her Hit Parade: Jackie Kennedy and Ari Onassis. "Melissa, JFK looked better on his way to Parkland Hospital than Ari did on his way to get on his private plane to fly to his private island to get on his private yacht. He was physically repulsive, yet he managed to snag the most sought-after woman in the world. And trust me, it wasn't his way with words that lured her to his bed; it was his way with his wallet."

Finally she brought the hammer down: Angelina Jolie and Billy Bob Thornton. "Yes, Melissa, now she's with Brad Pitt, but he's really just a trophy. She wanted someone that her kids, Maddox, Jimmy, Stevie, and Mogumbo, could look up to. Angelina Jolie is an absolute perfect ten, and Billy Bob looks like the kind of guy who isn't allowed within ten feet of a schoolyard. Honestly, if he weren't a movie star, and were just the guy living in the trailer next door, would you let him babysit? I rest my case."

I'd write more about this, but I'm running late. I'm going to have my legs waxed, my ears pinned, my eyes lifted, and my lips plumped. I'll be back in twenty minutes.

> **"Melissa, better to have a new you coming out of an old car than an old you coming out of a new car."**

I grew up my whole life hearing my mother tell me that if I (or she) didn't like a certain part of me, "don't worry; we'll have that fixed." On one hand it was an incredibly destructive thing for a young girl to hear, but on the other hand, at some point I realized that she was coming from a place of wanting me to be my best; even if "my best," in her opinion, was found in some doctor's office. There were times when it felt critical and mean, but sometimes I just have to admit that the old bitch was right. I do look better rested and more relaxed when I'm chock-full of Botox and fillers. Thanks, Mom.

Lock Up Your Virgins

PATTI STANGER HAS made a fortune as the host and creator of the hit television series *Millionaire Matchmaker*. This galled my mother to no end. Basically, because she'd spent most of her (and my) adult life trying to fix me up with Mr. Right (as opposed to Mr. Right Now). And not only did *none* of them pan out into any sort of long-term, committed relationship, but she never made a dime off her efforts. "You do realize that Patti isn't married, don't you?" she snapped at me one night while we were watching the show. I said, "I'm sure Patti's fine, and when she gets lonely, she can go to the bank and hug the hedge fund guy who handles her millions."

One of the biggest wishes in my mother's life was for me to be married and settled down with a good man. She was miserable when I was single—and considering that I'm forty-six and I was married for only three years, that leaves her with forty-three years of misery. I get why she wanted me to be married, or at least be with someone for the long haul. Even though she was a self-made woman, she didn't make the journey to the top by herself; she had my father walking beside her for most of it. She felt it was easier for a woman (or a gay man) to get ahead if there was a man to help balance her life and cover her ass. That's what she wanted for me.

Her search began on my first day of third grade. All the children in my school had to stand up in assembly that day and tell everyone a little something about themselves. Obviously the parents had trained them in what to say. "I'm Neil Conyers. My daddy's a doctor, and I want to be a baseball player." "I'm Tammy Levy, and I'm four feet tall, and I have a sister named Ivy." Then it was my turn. "I'm Melissa Rosenberg, and I'm single, and I'd like to meet a nice Jewish boy with liquid assets and a good nose." Some of the teachers laughed, and some were appalled. My mother just smiled knowingly and waited in the back of the auditorium to collect phone numbers.

Since I had steady boyfriends all through high school and college, and then got married, most of the damage to my mother came after I was divorced.

She tried and tried to set me up on dates, and it was awful and awful. It just never worked.

For example, once she called me and said she had met the most charming, successful, athletic, handsome man. "Can I give him your number?" she asked. I said, "Fine." She said, "Good! I already have. He's coming out to LA for work." So I arrange to meet him at a restaurant. I get there, and he stands up and walks over to me and says, "Hi, Melissa. I'm Dave. Your mother said we'd be a perfect match." Turns out she was right; we were a perfect match. We were both five foot three. Actually I'm kidding. I'm five three. He was closer to five two—maybe. And that's with lifts and standing on his tippy toes. We were talking about skiing and I looked down and saw that his feet were dangling off the end of his chair. I called my mother later and said, "Mom, what the fuck? You know I like taller guys. He's two feet tall!" She said, "Oh, I'm sorry. I didn't know. I only saw him sitting behind a table. I didn't see him standing up." I said, "Maybe you did."

Another time, she and two of her lesbian fans went on a mission to find me a man. The lesbians set me up on a date with a doctor they adored. They gave my mom his info. She e-mailed him to try to set us up on a date. He called her back and told her, "I have two rules: I do not date my patients, and I do not date women." Didn't faze her in the least. All she cared about was that he was a doctor. She used to say that visiting a sick friend in the hospital wasn't just a good deed; it was an opportunity. "You never know; you could meet a single doctor. Make sure you go in full hair and makeup, tight jeans, a low-cut blouse, and high heels." Ahh, the perfect look in a cardiac care unit.

In her world, being married to a doctor was the ultimate success, and if I wanted to marry a doctor, she felt I should put myself in a position to meet one. She used my cousin Andrew's wife, Laurie, as an example. "Melissa! *She is a nurse.* That's how she managed to snag Andrew. She got herself a doctor!" "So now I should quit my showbiz career and go to nursing school so I can meet a doctor?" She said, "Wouldn't be such a bad idea."

In hindsight, I feel I should've seen all the yenta-ing coming. When I was in sixth grade she took me to see a production of *Fiddler on the Roof* on Broadway. Every time the town matchmaker, Yente, hit the stage, my mother would nod, elbow me, and mutter under her breath. "*Humph*. Pay attention, Melissa. You're not getting younger."

(Years later she did the same thing when we went to see a revival of *Fiddler* starring my mother's good friend Rosie O'Donnell as Golde. Rosie was great, but her Yiddish accent sounded so much like an Irish brogue that my mother leaned over and said, "I didn't know Anatevka was a suburb of Dublin.")

As I write this, although I've started dating someone, I'm technically single—which would have made my mother very anxious. Mom, if you're reading this—don't worry. I still have Patti Stanger's private number.

When it came to my boyfriends my mother had no middle ground; she either liked them or hated them. The ones I liked the most she liked the least. Oddly, she seemed to prefer the rich ones.

The Purse

THE SEVEN WONDERS of the Ancient World are the Great Pyramid of Giza, the Hanging Gardens of Babylon, the Statue of Zeus at Olympia, the Temple of Artemis at Ephesus, the Mausoleum at Halicarnassus, the Lighthouse of Alexandria, and the Colossus of Rhodes.* I would like to nominate an eighth: my mother's purse.

A couple of years ago we were going through airport security and something in her bag started beeping, so the TSA agents pulled her over to the side for a security check. She didn't mind the pat-down (in fact, I think she enjoyed it and might even have tried to give the agent her number), but when they decided to empty her purse, things got ugly.

She didn't feel violated with a strange man patting her ass, yet one going through her purse was a step too far. She started in with "What do you think, I'm a criminal

---

* My mother had a joke in her act that the Colossus of Rhodes was really just Cee Lo Green doing a concert in Greece.

or a drug mule? That's right, I'm part of the famed Fin-
kelstein cartel and I've got a kilo of coke in my vagina."

First off, her purse weighed between eighteen and
twenty-five pounds. (Its weight fluctuated, just like my
mother's, depending on the time of year, her exercise reg-
imen, or whether she'd had Chinese food the night before
and was feeling a little puffy.) All women carry around a
lot of useless junk in our purses, but twenty-five pounds
is *a lot* of junk. Even the TSA agents, who have seen
everything, were shocked at the weight. (Can I mention
that my mother weighed only one hundred ten pounds,
so she was carrying around nearly a quarter of her own
body weight? No one ever believes me when I say she
must have had the physical strength of a titan.)

When they dumped the bag, here's what they found
(and I know this because they inventoried everything): in
her wildly overstuffed wallet (besides the obvious driver's
license, credit cards, etc.) were dozens of receipts, random
business cards from all over the world, discount coupons
from stores she would never in a million years shop in, a
dry-cleaning ticket from 2006, and so many one-dollar
bills that I thought that she was pole dancing at a senior
citizens' home in Great Neck. This entire apparatus was
held together by a frayed rubber band.

Also in the purse? More loose receipts, hundreds
of jokes written on napkins from airline lounges (both
paper and cloth), a box of Altoids, eleven loose Altoids, a
large makeup bag, a full-size box of Kleenex, three pairs
of glasses (none of which were the ones she was looking
for), one and a half screw-top splits of wine stolen from
airplane carts when the flight attendants weren't looking,

a half-eaten piece of cheese, and random one-hundred-calorie snack bags (usually partially eaten).*

They also found a single hair extension that she had pulled out during the day because it was bothering her, two bottles of the same color nail polish, dog treats, and the things all grandmas carry in their purses: Purell, hard candies, a tissue (this tissue was not included in the afore-mentioned full box of Kleenex), a living will, and an actual lace handkerchief ("Melissa, a lady always carries a handkerchief"). And, somewhere in the bottom of this, was her private "I can't find my" cell phone.

The most interesting item the TSA uncovered was a Ziploc bag filled with bacon bits and a small bottle of what appeared to be blood. (It was fake, but she didn't want anyone to know that. In her head, it was a vial of street cred à la Angie and Billy Bob.) She had carried this Ziploc since right after 9/11, so that if her plane were ever taken over by terrorists, she could throw the blood and pork on them, and they'd never get their seventy-two virgins in heaven. (Not that she believed in heaven or hell, but just on the off chance that they existed, and on the off chance she would be heading south, she was going to make sure that that motherfucker terrorist from Al Qaeda would be riding that same train with her.)

This was her usual everyday purse. Don't ask about

---

* The food items were kept in a foil-lined pocket she had in her bag. She told me she had learned this trick when she was a little girl from her aunt Fay. She said Aunt Fay liked to steal food from restaurants, and she had a brown purse that was totally empty and lined with silver foil. She said when Aunt Fay came for dinner, if she had the brown purse with her it meant they were going out as opposed to eating in.

the travel bag; I simply don't have that kind of time. By the way, the beeping sound that set off this whole episode was coming from a Miracle Ear she'd found in her seat cushion on a flight she took weeks before and had forgotten to turn in to the airport Lost and Found.

P.S. When we finally got on the plane I asked her what her inspiration was for the giant purse, and she said, *Felix the Cat*. For those of you under a certain age, Felix the Cat was an old TV cartoon character who schlepped a "magic bag of tricks" with him everywhere he went. (Google him.) As was the case with most animated characters, Felix was constantly finding himself in strange predicaments he couldn't get out of. His bag contained *everything* and anything: ladders, motorcycles, disguises, guns, food—whatever was needed to free Felix from the tight spot he was in and move the story forward. At first I found this odd, but when I thought about it, it made perfect sense. First of all, Felix must have been gay, and you know how much my mother loved the gays. No straight man, or cat, not even the really sexually secure European ones, will publicly carry a pocketbook, a purse, or a murse. Secondly, Felix's magic bag looked like it was Louis Vuitton. Since the show was animated, it was hard to tell if the bag was real or a knockoff, but either way, I'm not surprised it caught my mother's attention. It also explains why she made me watch that cartoon every Saturday morning, way past the age when I would have found it interesting. Another subtle life lesson.

Dr. Frankenstein
and the Red Carpet Monster

WHEN MY MOTHER and I turned the award show red carpet into the RED CARPET in 1995, we had no idea
we were creating a brand that would become as
Americana as apple pie, ice cream, and Kim Kardashian's
ass. If we had, we'd have been sittin' pretty, instead of
hawking tchotchkes on QVC.*

That year neither one of us had much going on. My
mom was between gigs, and I had done a talk show pilot

---

* Things we didn't think of when we were creating the red carpet
shows, and that continue to haunt my dreams at least every ten days,
and during award season virtually every three hours: We didn't copy-
right, trademark, brand, or even figure out a way to charge admis-
sion to the carpet. We never thought to start a fantasy fashion sports
book, where people could bet on who was going to win what (which
designer will win, which star will win, etc.). We never thought to get
sponsorship from Dyson vacuums. You wouldn't believe the shit the
stars leave in their wake when they walk the red carpet. It's easy to
be a Monday morning quarterback and play the "coulda', woulda',
shoulda'" game, but the truth is, we loved every minute of every red
carpet event and are proud to have created it.

that hadn't gotten picked up. Then one of the executives at E! called my mother and asked her if she wanted to do live interviews at *The Golden Globes*. She said, "Sure!" Then: "How much?" When they told her, she said, "Sure-ish." (I believe this is when she coined the phrase "You can't spell cheap without E!" which she used to say on air at any given opportunity. We were live; what could they do about it?) At that time, the red carpet was nothing more than a photo op of famous people walking into a building. We were lucky enough to be the ones who turned walking into a building into an event. That first year, my mother's partner was the late Eleanor Mondale. Their chemistry was fine but not natural, because they didn't know each other and had never met prior to that. So when E! decided to broadcast the Oscars later that year, my name came up.

I had already been on-air talent at MTV and had served as a correspondent for *CBS This Morning*. I was also the second choice for what would become *The Ricki Lake Show*,* so I was something of a known commodity. (FYI, I adore Ricki Lake, who is one of the loveliest people I know.)

The execs at E! called my mother once again, this time to ask her if she thought *I'd* be interested in doing the red carpet show with her. Earlier that week I must've committed some awful transgression against her wishes, like cutting my bangs,† so her answer to E! was a very terse "I

---

* FYI, I was also the second choice for the lead prisoner in *Oz*, the third Real Housewife of Beverly Hills, and the fifth-youngest Von Trapp Family singer.

† Apparently bangs were a hot-button topic for my mother. In one of

have no idea what she wants to do or what she's thinking. You're going to have to ask her yourself; apparently my opinion doesn't matter. Besides, she doesn't listen to anything I say anyway. And if I ask her she'll probably say no just to spite me."

(And that is how the sweet, heartwarming story of *Joan & Melissa* came to be.)

But I said yes, and we started the wheels rolling on what has become, years later, a television locomotive.

One of the first things we had to do was figure out what kind of show we were doing. It was a red carpet, not a yellow brick road, so we had to ask real questions, not Hollywood fantasy pabulum. We also knew that even though we both had interviewing experience, we weren't trained journalists, so we couldn't ask probing questions of international importance. (We didn't want to make amateur mistakes, like telling people we'd been shot down in a helicopter while covering the war in Iraq when we hadn't been.) My mother and I were well aware that even the biggest stars might be nervous, trying to (a) not say something stupid and (b) remember to act sincere when they said, "Oh, it's just an honor to be nominated," so we figured the best way to calm them down was to have fun ourselves. We decided to treat the whole event like a giant cocktail party, with good conversation, funny quips, and bitchy asides and hope the audience found it as much fun as we did. And even though we were working, we always had fun. Part of the reason we had such a good

---

the last conversations we ever had, she said, "Melissa, get your bangs off of your face. You look like a sheepdog, and when people can't see your eyes they think you're shifty."

time was that my mother and I had a natural rhythm (one that got even better through the years), we trusted each other creatively, and we knew our roles. Since no one could out-funny Joan Rivers, we "decided" to let her be the funny one and I'd play it straight. Talk about a no-brainer.

After a while, our act was so well known that you could just say "Joan and Melissa" and people knew what they were getting.* And in time, the red carpet shows became more important (and more watched) than some of the events themselves. So, to E! I say, "Thank you." And "You're welcome."

---

* I'm lost as a performer right now, but I will find my own voice. I was taught by the best.

When we started our red carpet shows, we didn't have a clue that the simple question "Who are you wearing?" would make the red carpet more important for designers than Fashion Week or the September issue of Vogue. At the time, we did not realize that having an A-list celebrity in a gown would be worth more to a designer than a million dollars in advertising. Had we realized that, we could've made celebrities wear branded jumpsuits just like they do in NASCAR. We could have sold ad space on limos once we created Limo Cam. ("Cameron Diaz, brought to you by Prilosec!") Hell, we could have sold ad space on Christina Hendricks's cleavage. Ahh, hindsight is 20/20. (Or, in Christina's case, 40 DD.)

The Red Carpet Means You've Made It!

THINK MOST people don't realize they're doing something transformative while they're doing it; it's usually the passage of time that allows them to see the impact of what they've done. There are exceptions to that rule, I'm sure. I'm guessing Neil Armstrong knew that walking on the moon was a pretty big deal when he took that first small step for man. I'll assume Thomas Edison realized he'd done something important when all of a sudden he wasn't bumping into his furniture in the dark. And I'll bet Ray Kroc figured he was on to something when he invented the Big Mac and three weeks later America was filled with tens of thousands of morbidly obese children. But my mother and I didn't realize the red carpet had become a rite of passage for celebrities until Sofia Coppola mentioned it to me at a party in Cannes.

And once the celebrities realized that Joan and Melissa's red carpet was a destination, they were usually available and ready.

There were two kinds of celebrities who made the red carpet fun. The first group was what we called the brand-new "baby celebs." They were the new kids in Hollywood who were genuinely excited to be there. One of my favorite moments was at *The Golden Globes* the year of *Good Will Hunting*. Matt Damon and Ben Affleck were the two happiest, most excited, couldn't-believe-their-good-fortune kids in a candy store guys I'd ever seen. You couldn't not love them, and my mother and I did.

Another year, the aforementioned Ben Affleck (post-Gwyneth, pre J-Lo, which in his personal timeline is known as the "fun years") took my microphone and ran up and down the red carpet, trying to interview people. After a few minutes of frustration, he came back and said, "Holy shit, that's hard!"

One year, it was freezing and I was in a very short, weather-inappropriate dress (one that I'm sure my mother had made me wear, the better to snag a wayward het-erosexual actor with marital woes and a nice IRA). At a certain point, George Clooney and Noah Wyle, who were starring in *ER* at the time, came down the carpet together. (Insider tip: you can always see how a cast of a show really feel about one another by how they arrive. First year, big group, all-for-one, one-for-all. Year two, it starts to become a little cliquish. By year three, the only words they speak to one another are the ones that are scripted for them. Don't believe me? Watch an awards preshow.) Anyway, I was freezing, and they both offered me their coats. I didn't take either one. In hindsight? Stupid, stupid, stupid. (My mother said, "Do you know the resale value of that?")

The second group of great red carpet celebrities is the A-Listers, because they play ball. Even if they don't enjoy it, they pretend to. Most of them liked chatting with us, and they knew it would be a fun interview.

Sir Ian McKellen always has fun on the red carpet. He has absolutely no respect for rules or authority. (Any wonder why we liked him?) At one award show, he came walking down the red carpet smoking a cigarette. He got to my position during a commercial break. I guess I must have been staring at his cigarette covetously, because he offered me a drag. I said, "I wish, but smoking isn't allowed in public spaces in Los Angeles." He said nothing, but smiled and gave me that "What the fuck are they going to do to me? I'm a sir" look. I took a drag.

Julia Roberts and Sarah Jessica Parker were two of my mom's favorites. They always knew they were on the carpet to have fun. They'd come right up to her and say, "Okay, let's get this over with. Just say it to my face; tell me right now what you think of what I'm wearing."

One year after Sarah Jessica asked my mother that question, my mom actually said to her, "Honestly? Love the dress, hate the shoes." It was a classic Joan Rivers moment.

The only time I ever remember my mother speechless was when Denzel Washington came up to her at the Oscars and told her that he had been watching the show while he was getting ready and he quoted his favorite joke of hers back to her. I think in that moment it finally dawned on her that people were actually watching the show, not just six gay guys and a couple of menopausal women who hadn't heard from their kids in a month.

The most difficult celebs fall into one of two categories. I refer to the first one as "third down in an ensemble show or movie." The second group is made up of stars who hate doing the red carpet yet are contractually obligated to do it.

The first category is usually driven by the insecurity and bitterness and anger that only third-billed actors have because they are not the "star." They are defensive and snotty and feel they are above talking to the press on such a banal thing as the red carpet. They consider themselves so far above it that they are usually temperamental and annoying—and terrible interview subjects. They are the ones who refer to themselves as ar-*tistes*. I like to refer to them as ass*holes*. (We all know who they are, but in an ironic twist of fate—at least that's what my lawyers told me to say—I can't come up with any of their names. Hmmmm. 'Nuff said.)

The second category of difficult celebrity has a poster child. And that child is Tommy Lee Jones. The second he steps out of his limo and sets foot on the red carpet, you can feel the wave of dread passing through the press line, because you know it's not going to be fun, it's not going to be pleasant, and you'll be lucky if you come away with only a mild case of PTSD. Seriously, you can hear the Valium bottles pop open as soon as he's within a hundred yards of the cameras and mikes. So, I want to take this opportunity to send a message to Mr. Jones. Please think of this, if you will, as an open letter (add throat-clearing sound effect, here):

Dear Mr. Jones,

Let me start by telling you what an enormous fan I am of your work. In my opinion, you are truly one of the most brilliant actors of your generation. I also respect the fact that you, like me, are an Ivy League graduate. Granted, my roommate, Holly Litvak from Cherry Hill, New Jersey, was definitely not as cool as your roommate, Al Gore. (Quick question: Did you help him invent the Internet? Just curious.)

I also appreciate the fact that you are an athlete, specifically, an accomplished polo player. I, too, am an athlete, an accomplished equestrian in the discipline of show jumping. Did you know we had so much in common? Crazy, huh?

That being said, I understand and appreciate that you do not like doing interviews of any kind, especially those on a red carpet. However, doing these interviews is part of your job, just like interviewing you is part of mine. So here is my question: Why the fuck are you making it so difficult for us to do our jobs? You hate it and seem determined to make us hate it, too. What's that all about? Why spread misery? Look, we're all just trying to earn a paycheck, and mine, I'd like to point out, is about one-one-hundredth of yours. Also, smiling every now and again wouldn't fucking hurt! When *you* show up at an awards show, it's usually because *you* were nominated. Seriously, it can't suck that bad. You're nominated for an Oscar. You're walking down the red carpet into a ceremony at which you'll wait for your name to be called, not walking down the hall to the death chamber waiting for the governor to call. (By the way, have you ever done that in any of your movies? I'm sure you'd be good in the role of a convict or governor. You should give it some thought.)

In conclusion, I hope you do not take offense at my expressing my opinion. I'm very much looking forward to seeing you at the next Penn-Harvard alumni mixer.

Sincerely, your friend,

Melissa

One of the great lessons my mother taught me about show business was, "In this business you have to know your place. Your level of difficulty to work with cannot exceed the level of money you can make for others."

Know When to Fold 'Em

THINK COUNTRY singer/chicken monger Kenny Rogers said it best:

> *You've got to know when to hold 'em*
> *Know when to fold 'em*

Kenny is a very wise man. Not wise enough to find a plastic surgeon who used a scalpel instead of a blowtorch, but wise enough when it came to gambling. And when it came to gambling, my mother took Kenny's advice.

Before you all go down that "Oh, maybe the reason Joan worked so hard is because she pissed away a fortune playing the ponies and was up to her eyes in debt" road, please note, that's not the case; my mother pissed away a fortune on expensive jewelry and designer clothes.

My mother took Kenny Rogers's advice about knowing when to fold 'em. She believed you had to know which battles you should fight and which ones you shouldn't, which wars could be won and which couldn't. She also knew (and taught me) when and how to fight for jobs, money, and creative control. She used to say, "You can only be as demanding as your star power allows."

For example, Barbra Streisand has the reputation for being a diva. Barbra Streisand also has Oscars, Grammys, Emmys, and Tonys, and delivers number one albums and sells out arenas. If she wants to be a diva, she can get away with it. Katherine Heigl, on the other hand—I know what you're thinking: "Who the fuck is Katherine Heigl?" My mother's point exactly.*

For those of you who don't consider TMZ the most important news outlet in the world (and you should be ashamed of yourselves if you don't), here's the backstory of the most recent tale of Divas Gone Wild. Katherine Heigl was one of the original members of the ensemble cast of *Grey's Anatomy,* which debuted in 2005 and is *still* going strong in its eleventh season. Katherine was one of the breakout stars of the show and even won an Emmy for Best Supporting Actress. Then she apparently became demanding and difficult to work with, even turning down another Emmy nomination because, as she publicly stated, she didn't think the show's writing was good enough for her to be nominated. At that exact same time, she capitalized on her television success and started making feature films, the most successful of which was Judd Apatow's big hit *Knocked Up.* After a few more movies, which were not nearly as successful as *Knocked*

---

* When Comedy Central roasted my mother, Tom Arnold had a great joke. He said, "Joan Rivers is a diva. A diva is what you call a cunt when she's still in the room." Five years later, still funny.

Up, Katherine began taking swipes at the movie that had made her a star.

Then, magically, she stopped working for the next five years, and I'm pretty sure it wasn't her choice. As my mother advised me when all this was going down, "Melissa, never burn a bridge while you're still on it."* That's a very good piece of advice. I think I'll share it with Lindsay Lohan . . . and Gwyneth Paltrow . . . and Shannon Doherty . . . and Lea Michele . . . and . . .

My mother also had little patience for pretentious phony-baloneys, which in Hollywood means everyone.†
Actors and movie stars are known for being notoriously grand (or, as my mother would say, "graaaaand") and filled with their own self-importance. I can attest to this because my mother was an actress.

In her book *I Hate Everyone . . . Starting with Me,* she talks about how the SAG Awards telecast always opened with a hand-held camera going through the audience and stopping at various stars, who would look into the camera and say, "I'm So-and-So and I'm an AC-TOR," with such gravitas that one would think acting was the most

---

* The good news is that Katherine Heigl's banishment from the business seems to have ended. She's starring in a new series on NBC called *State of Affairs,* in which she plays a CIA agent named Charlie. I hope the series is a hit, but if not, maybe she can spin off her Charlie character into a lesbian housewife and get a series on Bravo.

† Everyone *except* those people with whom I'd like to do business someday. *You* are not pretentious Hollywood phony-baloneys. *You* are smart, talented visionaries, and I look forward to collaborating with you on projects that will not only give voice to our creative muses and, hopefully, make the world a better place, but also make all the $tudio head$ and network executive$ happy.

important occupation in the world. She knew this was ridiculous behavior but not completely the actors' faults. After all, they spend most of their waking (and sleeping) hours surrounded by teams of gofers, fetchers, schleppers, lackeys, and sycophants, who tend to their every need and constantly remind them of how fabulous they are. It's easy to see how that kind of attention could make someone think they're all that and more.

Another (good) reason my mother couldn't abide people who were *graaaand* is that they tended to be humorless and took themselves way too seriously. And if you weren't funny or weren't able to get the joke, you weren't going to be in her good graces. (She had exceptions. For example, she didn't think doctors should be looking for a laugh. She used to have a joke in her act: "Dr. Schwartz, at your cervix!") The reason she loved the likes of George Clooney and Meryl Streep and Robert DeNiro is that they are in on the joke. They know they're talented, they know their work matters, but they know that they're making entertainment, not replicating liver cells to save lives.

This is as opposed to one B-level actress (who shall remain nameless because she's psychotic, she knows where I live, and I'm actually afraid of her) who forgot she was raised in a double-wide and decided she was an *artiste* of the highest order. Not only did she break into French in mid-conversation, but she also enjoyed reading poetry aloud, often pausing for dramatic effect in the hope that us simple, unenlightened folk could take in all that she was saying and hopefully grasp the meaning and the beauty of her words. She pulled this shit in front of my mother once. My mother, not one to be outsmarted,

waited for her to finish and then said, "That was wonderful. You should try reading it in its original Gaelic. So
much of the beauty is lost in the translation." Then she
turned to me and whispered, "Melissa, I'm all for people
bettering themselves, but please, at one point she needed
to be reminded she came from a trailer park."

The winner of the front-row seat on the Joan Rivers
Bullshit Bus belonged to Madonna.* (Gwyneth Paltrow
finished second and Kanye West, naturally, brought up
the rear.) In between Sean Penn and girlie-looking, His-
panic dancer boys, Madonna was married to the British
film director Guy Ritchie. One night my mother and I
were watching Madge being interviewed on TV about
some forgettable movie that she and Guy had made (and
I say forgettable because even I've forgotten it). To our
surprise, Madonna was speaking with an English accent.
And I don't mean a slight accent. I mean, "'Ello, Guv'nah!
Might you be needin' a wee bit o' bangers-and-mash?" I
looked at my mother and said, "Isn't Madonna from De-
troit? I know she's living in the UK, but what's up with
the accent?" My mother said, "Just be thankful she didn't
marry a pygmy. She'd be speaking a click-click language
and shooting poachers with a blow gun."

You know which singer keeps it real? Dionne Warwick. If you saw her on the street, you'd never know that
it was Dionne Warwick. She wouldn't be dressed how

---

* All joking aside, my mother really respected Madonna. She
thought she was smart and hardworking, and that she never backed
down. She also appreciated that Madonna was constantly reinvent-
ing herself—that's quite a compliment coming from a woman who
had 365 plastic surgeries.

you would imagine "Dionne Warwick" would dress. She dresses like a widow who took a bus from Long Island to Atlantic City to see "Dionne Warwick." (You know the look: pink sequined sweatshirt and matching baseball cap.) I'm not sure if she dresses like that by choice or by necessity; her financial troubles have been well documented. My mother once said to me, "You'd think one of her psychic friends would have seen it coming and told her to hang on to her money." But Dionne was being Dionne, and as my mom would say, "You gotta like that."

My mother always encouraged me to be myself. "Unless you're going to be boring on that day, in which case, do us all a favor and be someone else."

My mother at two. Even then she lied about her age
and tried to pass herself off as one and a half.

Yes, that's cousin Alan, and yes, he looks frightened because she's holding a knife.

My parents' version of beachwear.

The only time I was allowed to burp without saying, "Excuse me."

Genius at rest

My father told my mother he did his best work while sleeping, so she left him alone. I'm so proud of my dad; he out-manipulated The Manipulator!

Before the
Kardashians.

My mother took me everywhere, whether I wanted to go or not.

My first horse show in 1974. My mother was so proud and had so much fun that day.

Her enthusiasm was infectious.

The big time! Headlining in Las Vegas.

Here I am at age four, in Las Vegas, with my mother's BFFs Bambi, Trixie, Roxie, Bubbles, Kitten, and Bang-Bang.

(Left) Proudly displaying the job she loved most. *(Right)* "Melissa, I know I baked it, but there are photographers here; pretend you like it. You can throw it up later."

With Cooper, her pride and joy—you can see by the way she's holding
him there's no plan to let him go anytime soon.

Any gift given to Ms. Rivers will be donated unopened to Nazi Youth

Sign on my mother's dressing-room door, on her birthday last year.

No, we didn't get to keep the wardrobe or jewelry.

A pic my mother took of me when we stumbled upon an actual crime scene on our way to a shoot at Hollywood Park Racetrack.

Three of these people are dressed appropriately for a baseball game. One of them is not. Guess who's who?!

Swag the Dog

OF ALL THE award shows my mother and I worked on, none is bigger than the Academy Awards. Oscar night is filled with tension, drama, and questions, questions, questions. Questions like "Who are you wearing?" "Who do you think will win?" and "Who do you think will react horribly to losing?" But there's one question that's more important than all those questions put together: "What's in the swag bag?"

According to *The Oxford English Dictionary, swag* is a draped or sheathed piece of fabric. According to the Urban Dictionary, *swag* is an air of confidence, or swagger. And according to the showbiz dictionary, *swag* is all the expensive free shit that celebrities are given at award shows for no apparent reason other than their showing up.

Hollywood swag was originally created to lure celebrities to attend low-profile events. Let me clarify. I mean to lure *A-List celebrities* like Robert DeNiro and Julia Roberts, not "luminaries" like Teresa Giudice and the

Situation, who would show up at any event that offered baby lamb chops or free valet parking. Later, the swag bag began making appearances as thank-you gifts given to stars by TV talk show producers for appearing on their shows, even though the hosts had no idea who those celebrities were and didn't care about whatever it was they were promoting.

At some point the swag bag became a story unto itself, because the fancier and more expensive the gift items were, the more famous the stars who showed up. (Celebrities are like sharks; they're fascinated by shiny objects.) Soon, expensive, fancy gift items like Rolex watches, major household appliances, and all-expenses-paid vacations to private villas in Tahiti and Cabo and St. Bart's were filling the swag bags. My mother and I couldn't have been happier with this development. On one hand, we found it creepily bizarre that rich movie stars were being given expensive gifts they could easily have afforded to pay for themselves. On the other hand, we didn't care, because we would much rather have interviewed George Clooney than George Wendt, the chubby guy who played Norm on *Cheers*. (No offense to George Wendt; he's a fine actor. But the paparazzi don't give a shit what kind of dress *his* wife is wearing.)

This arrangement was a win-win for everyone—until the government decided that the rich and famous had to pay taxes on the millions of dollars in free shit they were getting for no apparent reason. Then, suddenly, magically, *POOF!* Just like eight-track tapes, workout videos, and Kenny Rogers's career, the swag bag was gone. (If you get very quiet and calm, you can still hear the sounds of personal assistants crying in anguish, knowing that the swag bag was no more.* The gravy train had pulled out of the station, and they no longer would be getting the free shit their celebrity employers didn't want.†)

The Grammys were known for having the craziest swag bags. One year, they included household appliances. I'm not joking: full-size refrigerators and washer-dryers. Interesting note: Almost every musician I asked about this was very excited to give the appliances to one of their favorite relatives, for two reasons: (1) Most Grammy nominees don't do their own laundry, and (2) even if they were so inclined, they'd be way too stoned to do it.

The Oscars always tried to have elegant swag bags, filled with high-end gifts and lots of face products: moisturizers, scrubs, toners, and scalpels. Included in the bag one year was a gift certificate for teeth whitening from a famous Beverly Hills dentist. The next year was a certificate for Lasik surgery. If you were around for five straight award seasons you could have had your entire face and body redone for nothing (which means some of the women would actually appear thirty-nine, and there might still be an occasional good part for them).

My favorite swag gift of all time came at one of the ESPY Awards shows in the late 1990s. To this day I remember that bag vividly: tennis rackets, sneakers, and other workout gear, and training sessions. But the best

---

* To be perfectly honest, the assistants aren't the only ones who miss the swag bag. I've been sitting shiva over its demise for five years now.

† At this year's Oscars, the swag bags were back, and glitzier and gaudier than ever before. You should have seen the smiles on the faces of actors and their sober companions.

thing of all was a year's supply of free Jamba Juice. ESPN, I thank you, and my abs thank you.

No one liked a good swag bag like my mom. It didn't matter what time of year it was, when that swag bag arrived she'd become as giddy as a kid getting a new puppy on Christmas morning. She'd gather everyone around the bag and open it, carefully taking out each item one by one. Then she'd start auctioning things off. It was like an episode of *The Price Is Right*. People would be guesstimating and bidding, and my mother would be like Bob Barker, except without all the animals and the pawing and the grabbing at the models. I'm not saying it would get aggressive or borderline violent, but I still have a small scar on my wrist from our longtime assistant Sabrina lunging at me for a coveted new bottle of Chanel nail polish.

Something in the Oven

Before I start the show I want to announce that the singer Adele has just given birth to her first child, a beautiful, bouncing baby boy. Sixty-eight pounds, twelve ounces.

—JOAN RIVERS
October 12, 2012, Royal Albert Hall, London, UK

O N ONE OF my mother's appearances on *The Ed Sullivan Show* in 1968, she was pregnant with me, but due to the network's broadcasting standards of the day, the censors at CBS wouldn't allow her to use the word *pregnant*. She had to use other words and expressions to explain away the maternity dress, big belly, and umbilical cord she was wearing as a belt. She always resented that, and from that point forward she hated euphemisms. So when I became pregnant with Cooper, I knew telling her about it was going to be a straightforward conversation, which is just as well, because if I had tried to use euphemisms, it wouldn't have been pretty.

If I had said, "Mom, in a couple of months you're going to hear the pitter-patter of little feet," she'd have thought there were rats in the attic or that I'd made a deal to rent the house out for one of those cable shows involving dwarves, little people, or folks who are just small enough to make us question.

If I'd said I had "something in the oven," she'd probably have launched into a rant about Heidi Klum or have gotten all crazy that "Betty Crocker isn't even a real person and that bitch is making a fortune selling cake!"

I thought about trying something sweet and funny, like taking her out to dinner and having the waiter keep pushing the *baby* carrots and *baby* artichokes, or having the maître d' bring a high chair to the table even though we weren't having dinner with Peter Dinklage. I also thought it might be sweet to secretly leave a "Dear Grandma" note in her purse. In hindsight, I'm glad I didn't. My mother was a stickler for grammar, and I knew that rather than rejoicing at the good news, she'd have started correcting my punctuation and usage. Last year, just for fun—okay, not for fun; let's call it pop culture research for *Fashion Police;* it sounds better—we were going through ads on dating websites to see how people were meeting and hooking up these days. Within five minutes my mother was correcting people's grammar. "It's *whom* do you wish to fondle, not *who*," and "Everyone knows there's no *h* in *bukkake*. What an idiot."

All kidding aside, I had a miscarriage before Cooper,

so when I became pregnant again, what to say, when to say it, and whom to tell were actually important issues. I decided that I wouldn't say anything to anyone for three months.

If I had told my mother too soon she'd have been following me around the house like a paparazzo following a Kardashian, and if I had told her too late, she'd have been following me around the house like a Jewish mother. Hey, wait, that's not funny. So, I decided that the best time to break the news would be when all our family and loved ones were together, because she was less likely to make a scene in front of people who would judge her but who couldn't help her career. In our family, a big get-together meant either holiday time or a bail hearing. (White-collar crimes, of course. What kind of people do you think we are?) And it was time for our annual Uncle Murray's Parole Hearing Brunch.* (Sadly, we're looking at at least another five years of this tradition.) Everything was going great—the barbecued kosher pork was delicious, the touch football was fun, and all the kids were enjoying Murray teaching them how to make a shiv out of a corncob—when I leaned over to my mother and whispered in her ear, "Mom, I'm having a baby!" My mother dropped her shiv, hugged me, and said the words every daughter wants to hear: "Is it your husband's? Is it

---

* Okay, okay, I wasn't at my Uncle Murray's parole hearing (I don't actually have an Uncle Murray, and if I did, he'd have a good enough lawyer he never would have served time for cooking someone's books). I was in a dressing room at E! when I broke the news that I was pregnant. And FYI, even though much of my life took place at E!, conception did not.

white?" I said, "Yes," and "yes," and "You have to swear you won't say a word to anybody." She swore she'd keep it quiet, and we both started to cry.

The next week, I started getting boxes of tiny clothing delivered to my house from her friends. I'm pretty sure they weren't for me, as even at my thinnest, I wasn't a Gap size 6–9 months.

Too Soon?

Comedy equals tragedy plus time.

—AUTHOR UNKNOWN

Tragedy is when I cut my finger. Comedy is when
you fall into an open sewer and die.

—MEL BROOKS

MY MOTHER LOVED Mel Brooks. He's funny and he's fearless, just like she was. Mel and my mother had a lot in common—and not just that they were both Jewish, both from New York, and both slept with Anne Bancroft.* They were kindred comedy spirits in that, for them, no subject was off-limits, no topic was too controversial, and no words went unspoken.

---

* I have no idea if my mother slept with Anne Bancroft. Personally, I doubt it. I can't imagine she would've cheated on Judi Dench. I just wrote that to see if it would offend people. I know it won't offend Mel Brooks, which was my point.

Over the past twenty years or so, my mother and Mel Brooks and George Carlin* used to speak out all the time that political correctness was killing comedy. Suddenly, and for no apparent reason, one day everybody started getting offended by everything. Shrieks of outrage and horror would go up from the hypersensitive masses, who were wildly offended by some joke a comedian told. It drove my mother nuts. "People are always yelling, 'You can't say this and you can't say that and, oh, you shouldn't say that.' You can't use the *C* word, you can't use the *B* word, you can't use the *N* word—at this rate we're only going to have two letters left. All I can say is, they'd better be *F* and *U*."

One of the things I learned from my mother was that good comedians push boundaries. She loved making her audiences squirm every now and again. In fact, I think the only thing she liked better than getting a huge laugh was getting an "oooh," followed by a huge laugh. My mother once said that if a comedian worked for years and years and never offended anyone, then she hadn't done her job. She pointed out that even Ellen DeGeneres, who's known for having a very gentle, nonconfrontational stand-up act, had the courage to ruffle feathers when she came out as a lesbian on her old sitcom. The day that story broke, my mother said, "Good for Ellen; I'm proud of her. Do you think she'll build me a bookcase?"

---

* Before George Carlin and Mel Brooks there was Lenny Bruce, who broke down barriers so other comics could speak their minds freely. Today, comics such as Bill Maher, Sarah Silverman, Chris Rock, Margaret Cho, and Louis C.K. are carrying on that tradition. And how can I not mention the funniest of them all, Sarah Palin, who makes us all laugh every time she opens her mouth.

I can't tell you how often through the years the self-appointed PC police would rant and rave, "Oh, Joan Rivers crossed the line this time!" First off, who appointed these anonymous scolds to be in charge of political correctness? (Last time I checked, there was no cabinet post, Secretary of Shit You Shouldn't Say Because You Might Offend Somebody. I'm pretty sure the First Amendment still covers comedians' rights to tell jokes. As my mother used to say, "You don't like the jokes, don't come see me.") Second, crossed what line? And third, who decides where that line is? The comedian decides, that's who. When you go to a doctor, do *you* read the X-rays and prescribe treatment, or do you leave that to him because (a) it's his job and (b) he's the expert?

My mother, like most great comics, knew where the line was. Yes, in the course of fifty years she crossed it occasionally, but she knew how far she could push the envelope. There are no hard-and-fast rules as to where the line is; it's an internal mechanism, an instinct. And the line is different for each comic. My mother could get away with jokes other comedians couldn't, and there are comedians who can get away with jokes she couldn't. For example, she rarely, if ever, told jokes about politics. Politicians, yes; politics, no. If you think about it, there is a distinct difference. It's not that she didn't have opinions on politics; she did. But as she put it, "Melissa, I just can't get away with telling jokes that are about politics, the same way Hillary Clinton can't get away with telling people that she and Bill still get it on."

Back to the quote I opened this essay with: "Comedy equals tragedy plus time." The big question of course is, how much time? For my mother, the answer was usually "very little." After my father committed suicide, despite my personal discomfort, the first night my mother was back onstage, his death was "in the act." By 9/12 she was writing jokes about 9/11. Was that "too soon"? Maybe for some, but certainly not for the woman who came up to my mother after one of her first shows in New York after the attacks and said, "God bless you, Joan. You gave me permission to laugh again and smile again. Thank you."

When I began my career as a television producer, my mother gave me a great bit of advice: "Melissa, when it comes to comedy, you have to be like Lee Harvey Oswald. You can't be afraid to pull the trigger." I know what you're thinking: "Lee Harvey Oswald? Too soon?"

I Love You … or Not

Joan Rivers's jokes don't bother me at all. She doesn't hit me where I live.

—ELIZABETH TAYLOR

WHEN I FIRST began writing this book, my fabulous editor and I were having lunch and I casually mentioned that when it came to making jokes about celebrities, my mother actually liked the stars she poked fun at. My editor thought that would make for an interesting essay, and I agreed. Funny thing is, when I started writing it, I realized that what I was saying wasn't all that true. My mother *didn't* like all the stars she made fun of. In fact, she couldn't stand a number of them, and many of them she didn't even know.

My mother was a comedian, not a poet or a social scientist. No matter what or who the subjects were, she was always looking for a punch line. She lived for the joke. In the 1970s she got a lot of press, both good and bad, for making fat jokes about Elizabeth Taylor. One night, when my mother was a guest on *The Tonight Show,* Johnny Carson asked her if she felt bad about making all those fat jokes about La Liz. My mother said, "No. I'm not the one shoving the potatoes down her throat."

The truth is, my mother *did* like Elizabeth Taylor. Not only did they work tirelessly together for AIDS research, but they also shared a close personal friendship with actor Roddy McDowall. The other truth is that they weren't all really Elizabeth Taylor jokes; a lot of them were just really good fat jokes that my mother attached to Elizabeth Taylor. Yes, some of them were Liz-specific: "Now that Elizabeth Taylor's fat, she's remaking a lot of her movies: *Cat on a Hot Cross Bun, Butterball 8,* and *Who's Afraid of Virginia Ham?*" But some of them— "She's so fat that when she pierced her ears, gravy came out"—could have been applied to any "plus-size" star. When Elizabeth Taylor died, Kirstie Alley showed up in my mother's act. And when Kirstie lost weight, Carnie Wilson came to the rescue. And after Carnie lost weight, Adele became the vehicle for the jokes.

I think one of the reasons my mother loved fat jokes is because she was a fat child, and viewed herself like that for her entire life. (She told me once that in grade school the other kids used to taunt her with "Fat, fat the water rat," so she figured if she beat them to the joke, it wouldn't hurt her so much.)

I can't even count the number of jokes my mother told about Chaz Bono, yet she and Cher, Chaz's mother, were always very good friends. Over the past few years, especially on *Fashion Police,* my mom must've told a million

Kardashian jokes, yet she had a great relationship with the family and we all get along very well. (My mother thought Kris Jenner was one of the smartest women in show business. I swear I can hear her shouting from beyond, "No, no, Kris! Now's not the time to leave Bruce, just as he's transitioning. If you had stayed, you'd have doubled your wardrobe!")

I think my mother spent 80 percent of her free time writing jokes about Nicole Kidman—the field of play was so vast: Nicole's tall, she's pale, she's rich, she's beautiful, she's Australian. Keith Urban's a hottie. Tom Cruise is a—I'm saying nothing; he's known for being beyond litigious. Anyway, you get my point. Then, one year, my mom winds up being seated next to Nicole Kidman at an awards show after party, and the next thing you know—surprise, surprise—they're friends!

It always annoyed my mother when she met the people she was poking fun at and ended up liking them.

Lest you think I'm going to keep waxing on about all the stars my mother made fun of but liked, don't worry, I'm not. This isn't the OWN network, where every story has a positive, uplifting message.

She didn't like Jay Leno. Her reasons were both professional and personal. On the professional level, she didn't think he was funny, and she felt that he'd ruined *The Tonight Show*. Comedically, she hated that not only did he water everything down to suit the lowest common denominator, but he telegraphed every single joke. There's a running gag in comedy circles that one night Jay Leno was throwing paper airplanes into the audience and one of the planes hit an audience member in the eye.

Someone yelled out, "This is the first time someone in Leno's audience didn't see it coming from a mile away."

Personally, my mother felt that it was unfair and deeply hurtful that Leno kept her off *The Tonight Show* for over twenty years for no good reason. After her death, Jay said he had banned my mother because he wanted to "honor Johnny's wishes." Hypocritical, to say the least, considering that Jay and his manager had had no trouble pushing not only Johnny out the door and off the NBC lot as fast as they could in 1992, but many of the longtime *Tonight Show* staffers as well. Wait, I stand corrected: Jay did have good reasons for keeping my mother off *The Tonight Show* all those years: first of all, she was funnier than he was; and second, he's a coward. Apparently Jay's cowardice has not abated since her death. This past December 10, eight weeks after my mother died, I was asked to speak at *The Hollywood Reporter*'s Women in Entertainment breakfast, as my mother was one of their honorees. Jay had been booked to make the welcoming remarks, and before the event started, I found myself standing not five feet away from him. Not only did he not come over to offer his condolences, as any person with a heart would have done, but he wouldn't even make eye contact with me, as any person with a spine would have done. It's too bad; it could have been a healing moment for both of us.

Although my mother respected Katie Couric as a journalist and a working mother, she didn't like her style. We were guests on Katie's short-lived daytime talk show, and rather than focusing on our reality series, which we were promoting, Katie instead went into attack mode. And when I say attack mode, I mean hammering my mother with questions along the lines of "Why are your jokes so mean?" "Do you consider yourself a bully?" and "Isn't it wrong to criticize other women?" etc., etc., etc.

It got so contentious that I could feel my mother's temperature rising, so I jumped in and started babbling about Betty Friedan's *The Feminine Mystique*, which my mother and I had recently written a column about for a magazine celebrating the book's fiftieth anniversary. Katie then threw to commercial break and promoted the upcoming segment, which happened to be with Carson Kressley, about what food to serve at an Oscar party! Given the tone of our interview, I was surprised that the next segment wasn't an undercover investigation of Gitmo.

As some of you may remember, my mother had a daytime talk show that ran for many years, and for which she won an Emmy Award as Best Host. She knew better than anyone what makes for good daytime TV interviews. They're fun, informative, and collegial. That doesn't mean that tough topics can't be broached, but the guests should be treated with an appropriate degree of respect. As every parent teaches his or her children, "It's not always what you say, but how you say it." (This is why Oprah was, and always will be, the master of daytime talk.) Apparently, Katie never watched *Oprah*.

I'd like to write more about the people my mother didn't like, but my lawyer is driving me crazy, texting me every five minutes, saying, MELISSA, PROMISE YOU WON'T WRITE ANYTHING ABOUT TOM CRUISE.

The Loo of Love

THERE'S AN OLD adage that says, "Neurotics build castles in the sky, and psychotics live in them." My mother would never have gone into them because the bathrooms were probably filthy.

As much of a public figure as my mother was, actually physically touching the public wasn't on her list of things she needed to do. She loved people; she was just a bit of a germophobe. Not on the level of Howie Mandel or Donald Trump, who, I believe, boil their hands three times a day, but she did have a designer hazmat suit in her closet.

She actually carried full-size cans of Lysol in her purse, along with multiple bottles of Purell and various brands of wipes. One would have thought she was planning to diaper a thousand babies or treat wounded veterans on a battlefield.

Whenever she entered a hotel, she would spritz and spray every single surface in the room before she took off her coat or sat down. At the end of her stay, her room was so clean the maids would leave *her* a tip. (Yet she had no problem eating a handful of M&M's from a Costco-size bowl on some receptionist's desk in a doctor's office.)

She especially hated public bathrooms—and by "public bathroom," I mean any bathroom not used exclusively by her, Cooper, or me. She was phobic about anybody else's yuckiness—if the person wasn't related to her. She had a clause in all of her contracts that her dressing rooms had to have a private bathroom and that no one else could have access to it.

She tried to avoid using public bathrooms at all costs. When I was little and was on the road with her, going from town to town by car, she had a rule: no food or water for at least twelve hours before we left the house, so we wouldn't have to stop. If she had back-to-back gigs, that kind of fasting was quite a challenge. I think we were the only Jews who observed Ramadan.

On the rare occasion when she did have to use a public or semi-public bathroom (office, studio), she would make someone (me, if I was available) stand guard outside the door so no one else could come in while she was in there. And once she was inside, it became lengthy sentry duty. For the first ten minutes you'd hear the sounds of spritzing and spraying and water running. Then, when she was finished cleaning the place, it was another ten minutes of the same sound effects before she tried to get out, which was an ordeal unto itself. That's because, afterward, she refused to touch anything with her hands, which meant she had to do everything (turn handles, open the door, etc.) with her elbows, knees, or feet.

She used to have a bit in her act about papering the

toilet seats in public bathrooms: "Every woman in this room has spent one third of her life in a public restroom going, 'Paper, paper, paper, paper, paper,'" and she'd mime covering a toilet seat. "Then you turn around fast and all the paper, paper, paper, paper, paper blows off and it's 'Aw shit, you gotta start all over again.'"

There are only two things that could have made the public bathroom scenario worse for her:

1. This is something every celebrity has encountered: a fan recognizes her, comes out of a stall, doesn't wash her hands, and wants to shake my mother's hand. My mom said that every time she saw that hand coming toward her, she felt like a car stalled on a train track with a speeding locomotive bearing down. She finally figured out a solution to the dilemma; she'd put the burden on herself and say, "Oh, I'm sorry, I can't shake hands. I'm just getting over a rash from an allergy." (Of course, she wanted to finish that sentence with "I'm allergic to filthy pigs who don't wash their hands after they take a dump.")

2. An even more uncomfortable situation was when a friend of hers would come out of a stall and not wash her hands. This would end lifelong friendships. "I've been friends with Claudine for thirty years. How could I ever shake her hand or eat at her house again?—Ohmygod! I had dinner at her place last month. What if she didn't wash her hands? Do you think there was pish in my meatloaf?"

The nice thing is that she passed these fears on to me. When I'm in a public restroom, I rush through so fast people must think I have the metabolism of a hummingbird. I feel like I'm in a horror movie and that a shark's going to come up from the toilet and bite me on the ass.

Even nicer? She spread the love to Cooper. When it was her day to read to the children at Cooper's school, before she started reading, she would play the "Purell Fairy Game" and wash the kids down before any of them was allowed to touch or sit near her. When I pointed out to her that Purell-ing the children might give them a complex, she said, "Don't be ridiculous, Melissa. They'll appreciate my care for their health and well-being. Besides, God only knows where those filthy, sticky, booger-riddled hands have been." (Yet she'd share a spoon with her dogs and justify it with an old wives' tale: "Melissa, you know dogs' mouths are cleaner than ours. They're practically antiseptic." "Yes, Mom, and later today we should wash our clothes on a rock on a riverbank, and then maybe birth a baby on the inside pages of a newspaper.")

I hope this essay will provide you with a chance for some self-reflection into your own personal habits. And when you're finished reading it, please go wash your hands. You have no idea whether the bookbinder was a slob.

From Here to Maternity

I **HAD A** horrible pregnancy. It was worth it, of course. Cooper is the greatest thing I have, or will ever have, in my life. There's no amount of pain and suffering (including water torture, bamboo under the fingernails, and listening to *Yoko Ono Live* on headsets) that I wouldn't go through again to have a child like Cooper. Although the grueling nature of those nine months does make me wonder exactly what kind of crazy that Duggar woman is. At last count, Mrs. D. had nineteen children. Nineteen. Someone needs to tell her it's a uterus, not a warehouse.

When I was pregnant, I had beyond morning sickness; I had 24/7 sickness. I would throw up in the morning. I would throw up at night. I would throw up during breaks from throwing up. I spent so much time in the bathroom, hunched over, that I'm surprised I didn't give birth to Quasimodo. In addition to the constant morning sickness, I had every complication known to man—including an enlarged prostate, which was odd, to say the least. I was so sick that I was on total bed rest for most of my pregnancy. I spent so much time in bed that my mother used to say, "Well, Missy, that's what you get for asking Sunny von Bülow to be your midwife." Had I not been so sick, I'm sure my mother would've figured out a way for me to make money on my back; it's not like she hadn't suggested it before.

To make matters worse, I felt really guilty being in bed all the time. Why? Because our family history is that my mother had the easiest pregnancy of all time and worked right up until the moment I was crowning. The story goes that she actually went into labor while onstage at a club in New York City. She was cramping and Lamaze breathing, but knew she had to finish the set in order to get paid—so she took a gulp and gave them thirty minutes.

So, anyway, I'm lying there, pregnant and weak, day after day, thinking I'm a loser and that I can't pull off what my mother pulled off (i.e., having an easy pregnancy and working continuously literally up until the moment I was born). I was constantly fighting with my doctors to let me get out of bed, out of the house, to work and be productive. And occasionally, between terrifying complications, they let me. I don't mean I took a job as a stevedore or a coal miner, but I did continue to work.

Guess who gets mad at me for doing what I perceived was expected of me? That's right, Mother Teresa Joan Rivers Rosenberg. On one of the rare days I was allowed off bed rest, we were driving home from E! and she started jumping on me: "Why are you working so hard, why are you driving yourself like this? It's not healthy." Here I am, sick as a dog, but trying to live up to this family standard, and I get flak for it. So I said, "You worked and worked and worked right up until the day I was born. That's what you always said. You led me to believe you were eight months pregnant, working on a chain gang breaking rocks in the hot sun!" She stopped for a moment and said, "Are you kidding me? Why would you think that? I slept all day long and I worked for half an hour at night. I spent the other twenty-three and a half hours of the day resting and being pregnant." Turns out, this is pertinent information she never shared. The moral? Never let the details get in the way of a good story.

Because I was having so many complications, they decided to induce labor early (two weeks). The doctor said, "When do you want to do it? It has to be in the next few days." I decided on Thursday, so I'd have a long weekend and give people more opportunities to visit and bring gifts. (I'm always thinking of others. Did you know that *Melissa* is Hebrew for "altruism"?)

On Wednesday night I wasn't feeling well, and since I knew they were going to induce labor on Thursday night, I figured I'd do what I needed to do on Thursday day. So I went to work, ran errands, and went to my yoga class. (FYI, Downward-Facing Dog isn't a pretty sight when a woman's in her forty-seventh trimester.) I was having trouble holding a pose. I thought I was cramping from the yoga positions, so I ignored it. After I had showered and gone home, I was still uncomfortable, but I remembered my mother saying, "Trust me. You'll know when you're in labor."

Since I have a very high tolerance for pain—again, another recessive trait—I didn't start getting nervous until I realized I was uncomfortable in five-minute intervals.

Light bulb! I'm in labor! So the entire family jumped in the car to go to the hospital. My mother, always properly dressed for the occasion, started putting rubber gloves on, in case she had to deliver a baby in the back of my Range Rover. To calm me down, she said, with a lilt in her voice (and how often we thought of her voice as gentle and soothing), "What are you so worried about? Childbirth is easy. Oh please. I had *one* shot of something and that was it. Shot you right out." Lying in the backseat writhing in pain, all I kept thinking was "How is it possible my mother went through this with just one shot of painkiller? She needs half a valium just to get a pedicure." I thought I knew my mother, but no, apparently I was a stranger in a strange land.

As I looked up at the front seat, squinting through my pain, instead of seeing a small blonde woman with stitches behind her ears, I saw Cerberus, laughing as it guarded Hades. Shamed and blamed, I gritted my teeth for as long as I could. Tradition be damned, as soon as I got out of the car, I gave in and started begging for an epidural.* Of course, we were in the parking lot and I was pleading for drugs to a valet, and all he could do was validate my ticket, but at that point I was desperate. Years later I found out that my mother's "one shot" was Demerol, and it was on an IV drip—for eight hours. Turns out I had shamed and blamed myself for nothing.

---

* Note to expectant mothers: Ask your anesthesiologist if there's any way he can leave the epidural in for the next eighteen years. You never know; he might say yes.

Begin the BAGuine

M Y MOTHER TOLD me that packing properly for a trip is a science, like physics, chemistry, and extortion. She said the key to successful, stress-free air travel is to pack "lightly." Of course, her version of packing lightly involved shipping containers, because "you just don't know what you're going to need when you get there."

My mother taught me never to check any luggage. She said that there was nothing to be gained by waiting around a carousel with a bunch of strangers. ("Leave that for carny workers and old perverts.") She was thoroughly convinced that with just a little more wiggling, she could fit virtually anything in the overhead compartment . . . or in the closet, or strapped into the seat next to her, or blocking the aisle. "Step around it. What, are you so important I should put my makeup trunk in the cargo hold?" When it came to the FAA rules for quick and easy travel, she thought these were nothing more than suggestions.

In case you're wondering why my mother travelled

with so much luggage that she needed her own personal Sherpa* it's because a lot of her bags were filled with products—Joan Rivers products (which, my friends, are available on QVC). She brought scarves and watches and bracelets and earrings to give out to anyone who crossed her path—and I mean *anyone*. Even when she went on safari in Africa, she had her "gifties" in tow. According to her, "You haven't lived until you've seen the smiles on the faces of those starving, naked Ubangi women when I gave them my classic Joan Rivers Bee Pin."† When I pointed out that these women didn't have clothes, she said, "Don't worry, they will. They're waiting for the UN airdrop. Melissa, just because they live in mud huts and eat sticks doesn't mean a little sparkle won't go a long way. Every woman knows a good accessory can update an entire outfit."

---

* Personal shout-out to Sherpa Babu Chiri. Wassup, bro? How's the fam? Miss you. Xoxo

† No, really, this is a true story. She gave them Bee Pins. I'm not kidding.

Do Your Duty(-Free Shopping)

MY MOTHER LOVED to shop. Anytime, anywhere, she was more than ready to pull out a credit card and swipe. In fact, one of her biggest regrets in life, particularly as she got older and her friends began dying off, was that funeral homes didn't have gift shops. This was doubly upsetting because she liked to wear basic black.

But this bit of shopping sadness was far outweighed by the fact that over the past twenty years or so, airports have turned into nothing more than malls with planes, and given my mother's travel schedule, she was never far from a cash register. The ever-expanding diversity of shops meant she could find anything she needed (or didn't need but just felt compelled to buy), from scarves, gloves, and five-dollar accessories to phone covers, snow globes, and massage chairs. She actually found her favorite rolling bag in an airport shop in Canada. Luckily, she spent a lot of time there and was able to acquire a full set of luggage in less than seven months. If those airports had adoption centers as well as stores, I'm pretty sure I'd have an entire litter of Canadian siblings.

International travel was especially exciting for her because not only were the airports bigger and as such offered more diverse stores, but they were duty-free. (A lot of travelers, cheapskates, and Tea Partiers consider duty-free shops to be some of the Happiest Places on Earth. The shops sell a wide variety of items at below-usual cost because they don't have to pay certain taxes on the merchandise. These stores are especially helpful if you're travelling overseas and don't want to bring a lot of extra luggage. Let's say you're a European man headed to New York City on a two-week vacation. Why pay a two-hundred-dollar airline fee for an extra bag when you can stop at the duty-free shop at JFK airport when you land and, for eighteen bucks, get twenty pairs of hideous brown socks to wear with your ratty sandals and mismatched shorts?)

To a small, Jewish woman with a large purse and deep pockets, duty-free shopping was simply heaven on earth. I'm convinced that at least once in her life, my mother spent thousands of dollars on an unnecessary plane ticket just to save six bucks on the giant Toblerone chocolate bar at the duty-free shop in Stuttgart.

Another thing that put a smile on *mi madre*'s face was the fact that duty-free shopping didn't stop at the Jetway; she could still buy stuff on board the plane. On most international routes, near the end of the journey, the flight attendants come through the aisles offering duty-free items for purchase. My mom knew that this was bargain-hunting time, because the crew was tired and could easily be manipulated into lowering prices or "accidentally dropping" an item into her purse. Her other fail-safe way to get duty-free items quickly and cheaply was to order them *very loudly.* "Do you have vibrators? How about triple-D batteries? What about salves and ointments?" The poor flight attendants were so embarrassed and ashamed that they'd offer my mother the entire cart for half price if she'd just stop yelling in that very distinctive voice.

Truthfully, though, my mother said that the duty-free shop serves two major purposes: First, it provides passengers a chance to buy a great last-minute gift for someone, to show them that you'd thought about them. (As my mother knew and taught me well, no one doesn't like getting a present, and no one doesn't like to know other people are thinking about them—even if they're doing it in a tax-free store.) Second, carrying a duty-free bag distracts the customs agents from going through your bags and looking for all the shit you actually are smuggling in. (Not that my mother would ever have done that, no, not her. FYI, she did not consider "muling" smuggling— and if you don't believe me, ask the guy she convinced to bring in a Chanel bag from Paris for her in his colon.)

A Dingo Stole My Baby

THE FIRST THING the doctors do when a baby is born is make sure that it has all the right parts in all the right places. According to my mother, that means nose on face, toes on feet, money in bank. Then, once all the parts are present and accounted for, they let you hold the slimy little critter on your chest for a photo op. Next, they hose it down and tag it, like it's an elephant they're tracking in Kenya. They put a tiny electronic wristband on the tiny wrist to make sure no strangers come in and steal the baby from the nursery. I think of it as a Baby LoJack.

Little did I know as a kid that I did not have to worry about "stranger danger." I had to worry about a small, blonde predator, usually camouflaged in furs, QVC jewelry, and Manolo Blahniks. Some of you might have known her as Joan Rivers. I knew her as Grandma Dingo. Cooper was less than six hours old the first time she tried to make a run with him. To be fair, she wasn't trying to abscond with him and take him to a Third World country to sell into the slave trade or put him to work in one of her jewelry factories. ("Little hands can set little stones!") She was simply going to the gift shop to buy a "Congratulations, You're a New Grandma" card for me to lovingly and sincerely sign. What she didn't realize was that the painted lines on the floors of the maternity ward weren't just some weird, random art installation; they were electronic sensors. If one of the little Baby LoJacks crossed one of those lines, it'd set off an APB and a very loud alarm. I don't want to say my mother disrespected the boundaries, but when she was on the ward, those alarms went off more than Lindsay Lohan's ankle bracelet.

She wouldn't let Cooper out of her grip; he was with her at all times, like her new favorite accessory. He was with her when she visited the hospital linen closet to find some crisp sheets she could shove in her bag and take home. He was by her side when she decided to have a cocktail party on the geriatric floor. ("You never know, Melissa, where you might meet somebody!") He was even in tow when she made a surprise visit to the dean of the hospital's medical school to inquire about her genius grandson's early application.

Once we got home, John and I began our journey as parents. We were amazed at the beautiful little creature we had produced. And my mother was amazed at all the new stuff she could buy for her new favorite family member.

Things had changed in Babyland since the fateful day when my mother popped me out between lunch and cocktails, and she wasn't so thrilled with some of the advances. For example, she had never used disposable diapers and had never seen a Diaper Genie, which she actually found fascinating. For those of you not in the Mommy Mafia, a Diaper Genie is a disposable diaper system that turns dirty diapers into what look like link sausages and keeps the smell to a minimum. The Genie's design is a white plastic countertop device. When she first saw it, my mother mistook it for a large coffee grinder. Needless to say, the decaf that day was a tad strong.

She'd never used car seats. (To be fair, when she was a baby they didn't have cars.) She told me once, "Missy, they didn't have car seats when you were born, and you survived just fine. I used to lay you on the floor of the passenger side. I would have held you on my lap, but I didn't want to wrinkle my blouse."

My mother was horrified when she first saw a baby monitor. She said, "Melissa, I do not like that *thing*. It's cold, it's impersonal, and it's unfeeling. It reminds me of your father. God, I miss him. Besides, what am I supposed to tell the woman I hired to sleep on the floor of Cooper's room, who has been instructed to alert us should he make a sound or a peep? Am I supposed to kick her out and give her a one-way ticket back on the raft to Cuba? Missy, I don't want to put this woman out of work. This baby monitor thing is killing the economy!"

In all honesty, from the moment my mother wrestled Cooper from my arms—I'm grateful she held a beat; it could have been worse; she could have wrestled him from my vagina—she adored him. No matter where she was in the world, not a day went by where she didn't call, e-mail, or text to check in on him and send him some love. I can truly say that, with all due respect to my father, all the men my mother dated, all the men she fantasized about dating, and Al Roker (don't ask), Cooper was the love of her life.

Murder and Mayhem

N ONE OF her last interviews, my mother was asked, "Who is your favorite character in literature?" She said, "Ted Bundy." I understand many of you may think that odd and assume she would have picked Joan of Arc or Jane Eyre or maybe even Hester Prynne (because she was slutty yet proud), but it seems perfectly normal to me. My mother loved murder. Not committing it of course, just knowing about it. She liked "being in the loop." In fact, reading books and watching TV shows about murder and mayhem was one of our strongest mother-daughter bonds. Tightly bound victims of horrific (and frequently senseless) crimes brought us closer the way I imagine porcelain dolls helped turn Marie Osmond and her mom into best gal pals. Lest you think I'm kidding, how many of you spent the night before your college graduation in deep discussion with your mother on whether it is possible to truly rid a crime scene of all DNA evidence?

How many of you reading this, when asked by your

mother, "Who's your favorite serial killer?" would have not only an appropriate answer but also one chosen from a wide and diverse field of candidates, of which both you and your mother had a working knowledge? I could, and did. I'll let you try to figure out which maniac is the apple of my eye and will reveal my answer at the end of this essay.

(And *no cheating*! The price to be paid for peeking might be delightfully gruesome. Here's a clue: he doesn't look like a maniac. Which takes Richard Ramirez, the Night Stalker, and Adolf Hitler out of the running. Richard Ramirez looked so terrifying that he *had* to be a serial killer; the moment he was born, the doctor looked at his mother and said, "Congratulations! It's a maniac!" And Hitler definitely looked like a madman.)

Reading true crime was a tradition in our home, like hosting Passover Seders or trying to figure out why midwesterners found Lawrence Welk so entertaining. My mother brought true crime to me when I was a child. In my really early years (pre-K) she'd read me traditional bedtime books like *The Cat in the Hat* and *Fun with Dick and Jane*. (Of course, she editorialized and said that Jane's emotional neediness drove Dick away and that Sally was the baby Jane had to try to save their marriage.) But once I was out of my footie pajamas, she let the games begin. I think I was in fourth grade the first time she tucked me in at night and sent me into dreamland by reading aloud from *In Cold Blood*. I think her intentions were twofold. On the one hand, she was introducing me to the great writer Truman Capote; how bad could that be? On the other hand, when I got a little older and became a tad rebellious, anytime I complained about how rotten my home life was, my mother could scream, "Really? What's so terrible? Would you rather be part of the Clutter family?"

My mother often said, both publicly and privately, that I'd made a huge mistake not snapping up one of the Menendez brothers when they were available. "Missy, they're *great* husband material! They're handsome, they're rich, and you'll never have to worry about getting along with your in-laws! It's a win-win-win!"

Interestingly, for someone who loved true crime, my mom was not interested in blood, guts, and violence; in fact, it sickened her, as it would most human beings, with the possible exception of the murderers themselves and maybe John Waters. I think it's the intrigue of true crime that appealed to her, the psychological chess match played between the perpetrators, victims, and the police. Or, maybe she just wanted to see what people were wearing when they died. I'm not really sure.

FYI, here's the actual list of the shows she had on her DVR in her home in New York City:

Wives with Knives

Scorned

Forensic Files

Lockup

Lockup Raw

And, of course, episodes of *Law & Order. All of them.* (She used to say, "Melissa, the only thing better than finding a diamond ring in a box of Chinese takeout is a Sunday *Law & Order* marathon.")

And here's an actual list of the reading material she had on her nightstand:

Hemingway

Tolstoy

Edgar Allan Poe

Ann Rule

Joseph Wambaugh

Vincent Bugliosi

The audio version of *Chicken Soup for the Soul*

These are strange reading and viewing habits for a woman who was afraid of everything and slept with *all* the lights on. When she was on the road, she'd booby-trap the front door of her hotel suite because she was afraid someone would break in, yet she would go to sleep happily reading about the Zodiac killer. Go figure. As a matter of fact, she loved sharing her true crime books. Last year, she gave the entire cast of *Fashion Police* copies of the new Charles Manson biography because it was "such fascinating reading, I couldn't put it down." (Note: since I just mentioned the Zodiac Killer, he's clearly not my fave; I would never tip my hand. Here's another clue: He was like a used car salesman; he worked on volume, volume, volume.)

Speaking of Charles Manson, one of my biggest regrets is that my mother didn't live long enough to see Charles Manson come thisclose to getting married recently.* She not only would have tried to pull strings to get invited to the nuptials, but she would have been green (hint!) with envy of those who got to attend, and would have made sure that Charlie and his blushing (or possibly bleeding) bride were registered at Hoffritz.

REVEAL:

And now, *mes amis*, the moment you've all been breathlessly waiting for—*my* favorite serial killer! (And when I say "favorite," I don't mean "Hey, I love your work," I mean "Hey, I love reading about your work.") Just like a Miss America Pageant without the swimsuit event, the competition was fierce. Do I pick Son of Sam, the postal worker who killed young lovers because his neighbor's dog told him to? Or do I go with Jeffrey Dahmer, the bland blond who let an eating disorder get way out of hand? I was leaning toward Gary Gilmore, the crackpot whom Norman Mailer wrote about in *The Executioner's Song*. The white trash factor was deeply engaging.

But, ultimately, my choice is Gary Ridgway, the Green River Killer—not just because of the sheer volume of his

---

* I think she would have enjoyed even more the reason Charlie's wedding was called off: turns out the bride only wanted to marry him for his corpse—which she planned on displaying (for money) after he croaked! Ahh, young love . . .

work, but because he met most of his victims in shopping center parking lots. This ties into many aspects of my psyche. It involves crime, shopping, and fashion, and it reminds me of one of my mother's parenting mantras: "Quantity is as important as quality."

Parenting a Parent

A S I WRITE this, my son, Cooper, is fourteen years old. If you think raising a teenage boy is a challenge, try raising an eighty-year-old woman.

My mother had always been a bit of a handful, to put it nicely. *Huge pain in the ass* would be less genteel, but it would be slightly more accurate—and I say that in only the most sweet, loving, because-of-you-I'm-on-Xanax kind of way.

There comes a point when an adult child has to start parenting her parents. I'm not talking diapers and sponge baths. I'm talking about dealing with parents doing what they want, when they want, with no regard for repercussions and giving you attitude/exasperated eye rolls when you tell them you think what they're doing is a bad idea. I reached that point in my life when my mother reached the point in *her* life when her answer to everything became "Yeah? I'm old. What are they going to do to me that they haven't already done to me? I've been up, I've been down, I've been loved, I've been vilified. Who cares what anyone thinks? I'm gonna do and say what I want."

For example, in 2008 my mother was doing a one-woman show, *A Work in Progress by a Life in Progress,* at the famed Geffen Playhouse, in the Westwood neighborhood of Los Angeles. Rather than staying at my house in Malibu for the run of the play, she opted to rent an apartment in Westwood. At first she said this was because she was an "artist" and wanted to be near the theater, so she could "stay in character" all the time. When I pointed out that she wrote the play and that it was autobiographical—she *was* the character—she said, "Oh, okay fine. I rented an apartment so Cooper and I could have some time together without you hovering over us like a helicopter, supervising me like you don't trust me to be alone with him. Besides, as a boy grows up, he needs his privacy." FYI, the boy was seven. Turns out the real motivation behind her wanting her own place was that, just like any other teenager—did I say that? What I meant was "slightly past-middle-age Jewish widow"—she didn't want to be under anyone's (my) watchful eye.

One night after a performance of her play, she met me at a local Chinese restaurant near my house. We ordered a bottle of wine and some dim sum and had a really nice dinner. At the end of the meal, I took home the leftover food and she took home the bottle of wine. We said our good-byes and went off into the night.

The next day, I get up in the morning and start with my usual routine: make sure Cooper is awake and getting ready for school, let the dogs out, put on coffee, and turn on the TV. But one thing that morning wasn't routine: my mother was in the news. Apparently, somewhere between the Chinese restaurant and her artist's garret, she had an adventure and didn't think to call me and tell me about it. For those of you who don't live in Los Angeles (and contrary to what many of the narcissists out here believe, most people don't), freeway traffic can be unmanageable, as it was on this night. So my mother was forced to drive on side streets. On the one hand, given my mother's driving "skills," that was a good thing; there are fewer targets on side streets than the freeway. On the other hand, side streets are closer to storefronts, light poles, and small dogs tied to parking meters.

Westwood is a GPS nightmare. The streets merge, they crisscross, and at times they go in irregular, circular patterns. At about nine o'clock my mother found herself in a crazy intersection in the far right lane when she needed to make a left turn. So she stuck her hand out to signal (not to request, to advise) that she was going to make a left turn—which she did . . . from the far right lane.

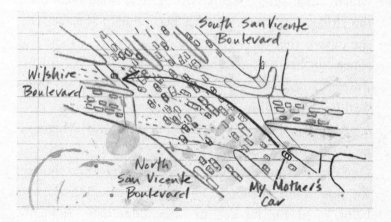

After an indeterminate amount of time or distance (three minutes? four blocks?), she happened to look in the rearview mirror and saw red, white, and blue flashing lights, which was odd, since it wasn't the Fourth of July. She realized it was the cops and they were pulling her over. To this day, no one knows how long the police car had been following her when she finally noticed the flashing lights, and since she liked to drive with the radio blasting at jet engine volume, I doubt she heard the siren, either. (FYI, this was during her Patsy Cline phase, so I imagine when the cops asked her to roll down the window, all they heard was "Crazy"—which is also what they saw.) When they asked her for her license and registration, they noticed the bottle of wine seat-belted into the passenger side—"Of course I strapped it in; it was open and I didn't want it to spill all over the floor"—and they assumed she was drunk by the way she'd been driving (not a big stretch).

The police made her take a field sobriety test—which, surprisingly, she passed. (Later, when recounting the story, she always made a big point of the fact that she passed the test—which she should have, as she was sober—in heels. Apparently she refused to take off her Jimmy Choos and ruin a good pair of Wolford stockings walking on the filthy street.)

After passing the test, she became Lady Magnanimous, thanking the officers for doing their job so well. One of them handed her a piece of paper. She thought she was about to sign an autograph. Turns out she was being cited for having an open container. Suddenly, Lady Magnanimous transformed into the Prisoner of

Zenda. She said, "It's not open; the cork's in it!" They said, "That's not how the law works." She said, "Can you please define 'open'?" They said, "It's considered open if it is not sealed." She continued this argument for twenty minutes—actually, she continued it for years and always maintained her innocence, despite evidence to the contrary: i.e., strapping the bottle in so it wouldn't roll around and spill—until, eventually, she wore them down and they let her go.

On the way home my mother called our assistant, Sabrina, to tell her what had happened and, even more important, to make her swear not to tell me. Well, after I saw it on TV, I called my mother immediately to find out what the hell had happened and why she hadn't called me. She immediately went on the defensive, seizing the opportunity to flip my reason for being angry on its head. "Melissa, I am an adult. I don't have to tell you everything." I said, "I know, but wouldn't it be awesome if I'd known ahead of CNN!?" Realizing her argument was flimsy at best, she managed to manipulate the facts to suggest that the entire incident was my fault.

"You know, Missy, if you hadn't selfishly taken the leftover food home for your child, I could have taken it and you could have taken the wine and none of this would have happened because you live only three blocks from the restaurant." Then she launched into attempted flattery. "We all know you're a much better driver than I am, Melissa. What are the odds you'll get pulled over by the cops around the corner from your house?" I told her none of this would have happened if she had simply left the quarter bottle of wine at the restaurant. She said,

"Are you crazy? Waste not, want not, Melissa. There are poor children in Korea going to bed sober tonight."

Then there was the hitchhiking incident.

When my mother landed at LAX each week, a car service would pick her up and bring her to my house. One time, in 2013, I believe, after a long flight, she was hungry and asked the driver to stop at the local supermarket so she could pick up a quick salad. She dashed in, got her food, and came out. Simple enough, right?

Wrong.

When my mother came out of the market she couldn't find the car, which the driver had simply pulled into a space twelve feet in front of her, rather than blocking traffic and waiting for her directly in front of the door.

God forbid she did what most normal people would have done: (a) look around; (b) pick up a phone and call the car service and have them call the driver; or (c) call my house and have someone come get her. But no, she chose (d) walk to the *very* busy corner of Sunset Boulevard and Pacific Coast Highway and stick out her thumb.

Meanwhile, the driver was hysterical, calling Sabrina because somehow he'd lost my mother. Sabrina was frantically calling my mother's cell phone, but she wasn't answering. Turns out the phone, as usual, was buried in the bottom of the abyss that was her purse. There was no chance of her ever feeling it vibrating, let alone hearing it ring. (The only time she ever actually answered her phone was if she happened to be holding it when you called.)

By this time, thirty minutes had passed and we couldn't reach her—we were all panicked. Suddenly, the doorbell rang and—voilà! There she was with her half-consumed salad. (I told you she was hungry!) She told us all about the Good Samaritan who gave her a ride to the house. I asked her how it could have taken her so long to get here, as my street is literally 150 yards from the market. She said, "I was distracted eating and chatting, and we missed the turn for your street." Then she marched into Sabrina's office and gave her the Good Samaritan's phone number, asking her to make sure he had two tickets for the upcoming taping of *Fashion Police*. I'm standing there with my mouth hanging open, and she's acting as if this were a perfectly normal ride home from the airport. I was furious at her—not only for scaring the hell out of everyone, but for getting in a car with a total stranger. I was so angry I yelled, "What's the matter with you? What were you thinking? You could have gotten in the car with a maniac or a murderer or a psychopath! You would have killed me if I'd ever hitchhiked." Without batting an eye, she said, "Well, if either you or Cooper had come to pick me up at the airport, none of this would have happened." I said, "What do you want from me? I was at work. Cooper was at school. He doesn't drive. He's only *twelve*!" And she said, "Whose fault is that? You should have gotten married earlier."

Not surprisingly, once again, she won.

"Melissa, dealing with an insurance company is like having sex with Jackie Chan. You're probably not going to get much."

Not Under My Roof

USUALLY WHEN MY mother came to Los Angeles to work or visit, she lived with me in my home. I expected she would follow the rules I had in place in my house—just as I was expected to follow the rules she had in place when I was in her house. (Who among us hasn't heard, or said, "When you're living under my roof you'll do as I say?")

Naturally, I was wrong. Even though my mother raised me to be a good guest, she was anything but. Basically, she ignored the rules she didn't like, which was a little disturbing because there weren't that many of them, and most of them were safety-oriented, not quality-of-life issues. (To the bitter end she insisted on running with scissors.) Obviously I didn't have to worry about her bringing strange men home, or doing drugs with her friends—is there such a thing as a Lipitorklatsch?—or turning the garage into a hookah lounge. I also didn't have to worry about her making a mess, because she was an anal-retentive clean freak. Seriously, my rules were really incredibly basic.

For example, one of them was "Do not feed the dogs from the table." She apparently had trouble with the word *not*. She was constantly feeding my dogs, Mike and Lola, from the table. My issue wasn't with her giving them snacks; it was the location of the snack giving. All I asked her to do, when she felt compelled to share her egg salad sandwich with them, was to put it in their bowls—not a huge request. One day I walked in and there she was, with the refrigerator door open, feeding them and herself leftover Chinese food. When I reminded her that she had promised not to do that, she said, "You only said not to feed them from the table. This is the refrigerator."

When she wasn't feeding them directly, she sometimes "accidentally" left food out where they could get it, like in her purse. Open. On the floor. Mike and Lola must've looked at her as a buffet with feet. Mike once finished the remnants of a honey-glazed ham that my mother had taken from the craft service table at E! It got to the point where I was terrified to leave them alone in the kitchen with her. Every week, when she was at my house, not only did each dog gain two pounds, but their insulin levels spiked dangerously. At one point I asked my mother why she insisted on turning my dogs into "Before" photos for Weight Watchers. She said, "They both have been fixed, have no sex life, so the only joy they have left in life is to eat."

Another rule that she chose to disregard was Cooper's bedtime. It didn't matter if I was home or not; when my mother was in the house, come 8:45, without fail, both of them would disappear. It didn't take Olivia Benson to figure out where they were, which was usually in my mother's room, eating some sort of sugary snack (that the dogs seemed to be enjoying as well) while deeply engrossed in something on TV. At 9:15, I would go downstairs and tell everyone it was time to wrap it up and that Cooper had to go to bed. I'd go back upstairs assuming that my mother would send him up to bed. Thirty minutes later I'd go into his room to say good night—no Cooper. So back downstairs I'd go. "Guys, c'mon. I'm not kidding. You've got school tomorrow." They'd both just launch into "Can't we just finish this episode? Frasier and Niles have decided to open a restaurant." When I said no, my mother would start in with "How often do I get to spend time alone with my grandson?" I'd reply, "Every week! Please, he has to go to bed or he's going to be a nightmare in the morning." She'd say, "No, he won't. Cooper, promise your mother you won't be cranky in the morning." Cooper would look up and say, with a mouthful of cookies and ice cream, "I pe9tjtn" (translation: "I promise"), and she'd say, "I swear I'll get him up to bed as soon as the show is over. Go to bed. You're looking very tired; don't worry, I've got this."

The next morning, when Cooper stomped out of the house exhausted and in a foul mood, my mother would look at me and say, "You know, Melissa, you really need to make sure he gets more sleep."

Forty Is the New Fifty

THE FIVE SCARIEST words that ever came out of my mother's mouth were "Melissa, get in the car."

There were very few things in this world more frightening than being in a car when my mother was behind the wheel, and that includes skydiving, swimming with sharks, and drawing cartoons of the Prophet Mohammed.

My mother was a terrible driver. I don't mean bad like "Hey, you're parked too far away from the curb." I mean like "Hey, you're parked too close to the couch." She must've taken driving lessons from Mr. Magoo. In her hands a car wasn't a means of transportation; it was a weapon of mass destruction. If the president really wanted to end the war in Afghanistan, he should have sent her over there to take a nice, leisurely drive. They'd have been waving the white flags in half an hour.

How bad a driver was she? You know how sometimes when you're driving on the freeway and, all of a sudden, thousands of cars start slowing down to a crawl and then stop for no apparent reason? *She* was the reason.

She believed that forty miles per hour was the appropriate speed for anywhere: driveway, school zone, left lane of the highway. Sometimes too fast, sometimes too slow—didn't matter. Her foot applied the same pressure on the gas pedal all the time. It was as if her right leg were bionic and was being controlled by remote control in a secure location by anti-American forces intent on destroying our economy by making sure everyone was late for work. One time we were driving on the freeway—I must have been ten or eleven, too young to drive—and she was in the left lane going, oh, I don't know, let's say forty miles an hour. Cars were honking at us and drivers were rolling down their windows and screaming and giving us the finger. I said, "Mom, don't you think you should go a little faster? All those people might be in a hurry and have something important to do." She said, "*They* have something important to do? We all have important things to do. So they're five minutes late."

She also had no problem driving with the hazard lights on. In fairness, she probably didn't know how to turn them off and had probably accidentally turned them on at some point, when she was fidgeting with the mirror to put on her makeup. When I explained that they might cause an accident she said, "Don't be ridiculous. I use them as a deterrent; that way people stay out of my way."

She also thought the lane lines were just for her. She felt that if you lined up the car's hood ornament with the lines on the road it was safer because that way you had plenty of clearance on either side. (That's why she always liked Mercedes; not because they were beautiful, fancy cars, but because they had huge hood ornaments that she used to line up the car with the road.) This was particularly frightening on two-lane streets. One day, when I was hanging on to the door, white-knuckled, she said, "Oh, Melissa, relax. Don't worry. They'll see me coming."

Temperature control was also an issue. She was always cold, so even if she felt the tiniest bit chilly, she'd put the car's heat on to blast furnace levels. I'll never forget the summer day she was driving me and a couple of my friends home from the movies. It must've been ninety degrees outside, yet she had the temperature in the car set at a balmy ninety-five. As she drove down the freeway, we were all hanging our heads out the car windows like dogs, panting for fresh air. When I complained about the heat, she said, "Don't worry; we'll be home soon." I said, "No, we won't. You're only going forty."

In California, where I grew up, it's state law that you have to take driver's education classes in order to earn a driver's license. So when I was fifteen, and trying to get my learner's permit, my mother took me out to practice driving. Once. The way she did it was, she would drive down the block and back, and then it would be my turn to do the exact same thing. She'd pick a quiet residential street in a senior citizen neighborhood for our practice runs. "I don't want you to be driving where there are a lot of little children around. God forbid you hit one of them. We'd get sued and Daddy would have to go back to being an accountant. If you hit an old lady, who cares? She's probably waiting for the hearse anyway. Tick tock."

When she was showing me how to parallel-park, she kept banging into the cars in front and back of us. I said, "Mom, you're hitting those cars!" She said, "That's why they call them bumpers." From that day forward, my father took me for driving practice.

Through the years one would think her driving skills would have improved accidentally, just by dint of living in LA and having to drive so much. But that wasn't the case. The more she drove, the worse she got, if that's even possible. Thankfully as she got older she could afford a driver, thereby making the world a safer place. (Again with the giving!)

Note: I was always very clear that she was not allowed to drive Cooper anywhere. However, it's entirely possible she did when I was out of town, and bought his silence with candy, toys, and cash.

Pillow Talk

M Y MOTHER LOVED to do needlepoint. She said it calmed her down. She'd get in bed, turn the TV on to Investigation Discovery to watch some dark tale about a gruesome murder, pull out her needles, and start sewing. How calming.

She liked to needlepoint pillows that had sayings on them that were either poignant or funny, or that had some special meaning to our family. Here are some of the actual slogans from her pillows:

> Don't Expect Praise Without Envy
> Until You're Dead.

> Birds Only Peck at the Best Fruit.

> Welcome to Joan and Melissa's
> Excellent Adventure.

> I Need a Man to Spoil Me or
> I Don't Need a Man at All.

I'd Rather Be Me with Only
Ten Million Dollars and a Lot of Friends Than
Him with Forty Million Dollars
and No Friends.

Glamour Has No Alarm Clock.
Fashion Knows No Pain.

Go Through Any Door That Opens.
You Don't Know Where It's Going to Lead You.

Say "Yes" to Everything!

Given her penchant for needlepointing while watching crime shows, I was always surprised she didn't have a pillow that read, PLACE THIS PILLOW OVER VICTIM'S FACE FOR 8½ MINUTES, APPLYING GENTLE PRESSURE. THERE WILL BE NO PETECHIAL HEMORRHAGING AND NO ONE WILL KNOW YOU DID IT.

I've Got a Secret

ULIUS AND ETHEL Rosenberg were executed by the American government for spilling secrets; the American people turned Joan Molinsky Rosenberg into a star for doing the same thing. Okay, not the *exact* same thing. Julius and Ethel gave atomic secrets to the Soviets in 1944. My mother blabbed about Elizabeth Taylor on *The Tonight Show*. Which bit of tattling had a bigger impact on the world? Most people today couldn't pick Julius and Ethel's photos out of a police lineup, but just last year my mother sold out arenas from England to Australia. You be the judge.

While my mother had an insatiable need to *know* all the gossip, you couldn't tell her any because she couldn't keep a secret to save her life. For example, there was one time at *Fashion Police* when one of my mom's cohosts was having contract problems. (I will not tell you which one, and you'll see why as you keep reading.) My mother, being the "newshound" she was, wanted to know everything going on in everyone's lives at the show.

As executive producer, I was privy to a lot of things, both professional and personal, that were, quite frankly, none of my mother's business. At least twice a week I would catch her lingering outside my office door, eavesdropping while I was on a call. When I hung up, she'd say, "Hey, I happened to be passing by your office—repeatedly, while you were on the phone—and I was curious: what was that about?" If I did not produce some sort of satisfying nugget for her, she would badger me until I just couldn't take it anymore. Sometimes I just made shit up to get her to leave me alone. That way, we were both happy: she felt that she was in the know, and I had some peace.

Back to the story. After one of the tapings, I met behind closed doors with said cohost. Nancy Drew figured out that if the door was shut, something important was being discussed. As soon as my meeting was over and I was back with my mom, the Inquisition began.

She'd badger me and badger me and badger me and badger me: "What was that about? What's going on? Is this big news? If it is, it's important that I know. As you know, I will be asked at the airport!" I told her, "Mom, number one, this is not huge news. Neil Armstrong landing on the moon was huge news. The Navy SEALs killing Osama bin Laden was huge news. This is nothing. Number two, and more important, I can't say anything. I'm the executive producer, and the cast and crew have to trust me and know that their confidences are safe." She said, "Missy, they *do* trust you, which is why you can tell me. I'm your mother. No one would ever fault you for telling your mother." Again I said no—clearly not the answer she wanted. She didn't see it as the end of the conversation; she saw it as a challenge, and she kept going and going and going. You'd think after all those years, I'd have been immune to her tactics, but you'd be wrong. The woman was a professional, grade-A, top-of-the-line, best-of-the-best master manipulator. After a good amount of time she just wore me down, like a suspect in the twentieth hour of a police interrogation who's willing to confess to a crime he didn't commit, just to be able to go home.

I said, "Mom, you must swear on all that's good and decent that you promise to never, ever, ever say a word about this to anyone. I'm serious. This is confidential stuff." She said, "Of course not. My lips are sealed. I won't say a word to anyone!" So, like a fool, I told her. We left her dressing room and within sixty seconds (and I'm being generous in the time here) we ran into the co-host in question in the elevator and my mother says, without missing a beat, "I can fix your contract issues," and for the length of time it took us to travel from the lobby to parking level P1, she proceeded to give detailed advice on how to solve this person's problem. We were in the parking lot and the stunned said cast member mumbled, "Thank you," and scurried off to the left as we headed to the right. Furious, I said to my mother, "You *swore* you wouldn't say anything. Do you know that now I'm in trouble, as is the person who told me details even *I* wasn't supposed to know? I can't believe you just did that!" Her reply? "Well, then you shouldn't have told me."

Her idea of keeping a secret was not what you or I

would consider keeping a secret. She thought there was no problem sharing a story about someone as long as the person she was sharing it with had no affiliation with the person the story was about. For example, if I told her that one of my neighbors was having an affair with a *very* married executive at ABC, she'd make sure that she shared this bit of information only with people who worked at CBS, NBC, Fox, and Showtime . . . and maybe Netflix. (Her other default mode was "I only told Margie, and who's she gonna tell? She runs a nonprofit. Do you think the orphans she's helping really care that your friend Tina is banging one of the network's CEOs? I don't think so." Frighteningly, there is some logic to that.)

I think part of my mom's blabbiness had to do with the fact that she never had any secrets or skeletons in her own closet. (There was probably no room in there, what with all the Chanel and Valentino suits and millions of QVC trinkets, scarves, and schmattas.) Everything in her life was open for public discussion and debate—from my father's death to Cooper's birth, from her first nose to her last chin, from her being blackballed by Johnny Carson to her redemption on *Celebrity Apprentice*—so I guess she figured everything in everyone else's life was open for discussion, too.

I constantly begged her to dial it down and keep some things private. I said, "Mom, be a well, not a fountain," yet she went off more frequently than Old Faithful.

Customer Disservice

A LOT OF people don't suffer fools gladly. My mother didn't suffer them at all. One of her biggest pet peeves was incompetence (and incontinence; more on that later). People who were bad at their jobs, or didn't care that they were bad at their jobs, drove her crazy. In the United States there is, ironically, a strange phenomenon that many of these people end up working in service-oriented fields.* She couldn't fathom how people who were bad at their jobs not only got those jobs, but kept them—excluding, of course, the twenty-year-old blonde secretaries with mad oral skills. She knew how they got where they were: on their knees. ("Melissa, the road to success is covered with rug burns.")

In December of 2013, while on vacation in Mexico, I bought my mother a diary, which became the genesis of her book *Diary of a Mad Diva*. One of her first

---

* I have a theory that this seemingly unique American phenomenon was originally brought here by the French, along with the Statue of Liberty and the Croissandwich.

entries was about a series of phone calls she had with AT&T while we were in Mexico, regarding their failure to properly put her on the international calling plan she had asked and paid for. Needless to say, the entry was hilarious, but the actual experience was infuriating. She must've been on the phone—mine, not hers; her phone wasn't working, remember?—for three hours, with five different representatives, trying to get the matter resolved. Call after call, back and forth, over and over again, until the problem got fixed. When it was finally resolved, she said, "How is this possible? They're the phone company and they can't fix a phone problem they created? What the fuck is going on here? What kind of morons are they hiring? And where the fuck is my assistant, who should have been dealing with this?"

I don't know exactly where my mother's lack of patience with the ever-growing horde of incompetents began, but the first instance I recall witnessing was sometime in the late 1970s, when my parents were out promoting the movie *Rabbit Test*.* My mother had just finished making a promo appearance, and we got in the car to drive to another city for another appearance the next day. I was hungry, and even though we didn't usually stop for food, because afterward, at some point, we'd have to pull over and use a public restroom, about which, as I've already mentioned, my mother was phobic (see "The Loo

---

* When they were out on the road promoting *Rabbit Test,* my parents gave me an assignment to write something down about every city we were in. As the through line, I based it on my favorite food at the time: French Onion Soup, which I had in all forty-two cities we went to. Forty-two soups, forty-two Pepto-Bismols.

of Love"), my whining that I was "starving like a beggar in Calcutta" wore them down and they gave in.

We pulled into the drive-thru of some fast-food burger joint and ordered a couple of burgers. The guy on the headset taking our order said, "We're out of burgers." Before I had the chance to get hysterical, envisioning myself as nothing more than skeletal remains on the side of the road, my mother leaned across the front seat, practically pushing my father though the windshield, and started peppering the guy with questions: "What do you mean you're out of burgers? You only make one thing: burgers. Your name is Burgers R Us! How'd you run out of them?" He said, "Well, it was really busy at dinnertime." She barked, "Of course it was. It was dinnertime. It's supposed to be busy. Didn't you plan for that?" He stared blankly and gave us coupons for free meals for the next time we came (as though there'd be a next time). Then, as we drove off, my mother looked at me in the backseat and said, "Boy, is he bad at his job. He ought to thank God he's not a lion tamer. By the way, don't you worry, my malnourished princess. There's a waffle house right down the road. Let's pray they're not out of waffles."

I understand that not everybody can be the best in the world at their job. For example, only one dentist can graduate at the top of his class at dental school. That doesn't mean everyone else is at the bottom, but when you go to have a tooth pulled, wouldn't you like to know that your dentist's last job wasn't in *Marathon Man*?

My mother was not one to live in the past; in fact, she was one of the most forward-thinking people I've ever known. (Be honest, how many eighty-one-year-olds do you know who have Twitter accounts or make videos for YouTube or Vine?) She was not a curmudgeonly old "things were better back in my day" kind of person, but she did believe that, in recent years, basic standards (manners, language, job skills) had dropped, and what in the past would have been considered unacceptable had become the acceptable norm.

For example, there was a receptionist named Carol who worked at a TV studio where we taped a lot of shows. She was happily married to Ken and had an eight-year-old son named Danny. Carol was kind and lovely and nice—and had the grammatical skills of a foreign-born toddler. Every time we came to work, before we went into the studio, my mom would stop by Carol's desk and chat with her. "Hi, Carol. Is Danny having fun playing Little League baseball?" "Yeah. He done good." Nails on a blackboard. My mother would continue: "Do you and Ken have plans for the weekend?" "Yeah. Him and me are goin' out."

This would drive my mother nuts. Once we were in the elevator and safely out of earshot, she'd say, "*He done good? Him and me?* Why can't she speak properly? She was born in Denver, for God's sake. My gardener, who got here from Tijuana on Tuesday, has a better command of the English language. And somehow she got a job as receptionist in a major television studio, *speaking to people?* Arrghh!" We're not asking anyone to speak the Queen's English, but they could speak at least as well as Shakira or Celine Dion!

I think that a lot of my mother's hypersensitivity to

professional incompetence was because she worked in the entertainment industry, which happily rewards incompetence. (Please don't confuse the "entertainment industry" with the "arts." The "arts" are usually run by artists, i.e., writers, filmmakers, authors, painters, musicians. The entertainment industry is run by lawyers and accountants and executives whose lists of failures are longer than those of the guys they've just replaced).* There's an old (semi-old?) adage that goes, "Show business is the only business where talent and skill aren't requirements for success. It's nice if you have them, but they're not necessary."

Think about that for a moment, my friends. Are there any of you reading this right now who haven't watched a movie or a TV show or heard a song and thought, "How the hell is this idiot so rich and famous? If this is the best we've got out there, we really are living in a cultural wasteland."

My mother thought this *all the time*. She especially loathed unfunny comics, which is not only an oxymoron but, according to her, a blight on humanity. Before I go on, let me just say that I understand that taste is subjective, and what one person finds funny, another may not. But I was raised by one of the funniest people who ever lived, and surrounded by other *almost*-equally-funny people (if I wrote "equally funny," she'd strike me

---

* The Peter Principle is a theory in which the selection of a candidate for a position is based on the candidate's performance in their current role rather than on abilities relevant to the intended role. To paraphrase, it means, failing upwards.

by lightning and this book would be over right here . . .
No lightning?). Anyway, I am more than happy to defer
to my mother on the subject of comedy.

For example, my mother wasn't a huge fan of slap-
stick, but if it was well done she could understand why
audiences liked it. "I don't find it particularly funny,
Missy, but I know why they're laughing." She couldn't
say the same about Dane Cook or Ben Stiller.

Let me make a disclaimer here:

My mother actually thought Ben was a good director
who could tell a story, and not a bad actor, even though
she did not find him particularly funny. She said he was
funnier than Dane Cook, "but who isn't? I have stretch
marks that are funnier than Dane Cook." Had she not
had bad experiences with Ben Stiller, it's possible—not
likely, but possible—that she might have found him mar-
ginally amusing. But she was disappointed in him for his
lack of basic good manners. The few times they actually
met, he was both dismissive and rude. It wasn't so much
that he obviously wasn't a fan of hers. The problem was
that she had a long-standing friendship with his parents
(the great Stiller and Meara), and she knew he had been
raised better than to be rude to his parents' friends.

She used to tell me that she heard that Dane Cook
was "very nice," and she thought he was very good in his
acting roles. She just didn't think he was funny, and she
had literally no idea why people were laughing at him.
One night we watched one of his comedy specials on TV.
When it was over she said, "I don't get it. There wasn't a
joke or a punch line in the whole show. Yeah, he's a good

performer but he's not saying anything. There are no fucking jokes! And he's playing an arena!" I said, "Mom, don't begrudge him his success; he's tapped into something that his audiences connect with." She said, "Who's begrudging? I want his agent's phone number."

Fifty Shades of Cray

Joan: Melissa, it's easier to ask for forgiveness than to ask for permission.

Melissa: So you'll forgive me if I tell you I spent the weekend in a cheap motel room with the New York Knicks?

Joan: Don't be an idiot. Of course not.

M Y MOTHER HATED rules (ironic when you consider that Judge Judy was one of her best friends). Let me clarify, she hated rules for *her;* she had no problem with other people having to follow them. In fact, she insisted upon it. (Growing up, I broke the rules so often I spent a large portion of my teenage, wonder years in my bedroom, grounded for committing some horrific offense and adamantly denying it, even though I had probably done it. And when I say "horrific offense," I mean like wearing shoes on the carpet (which of course I'd been asked not to do ten thousand times. Ahh, being a teenager.)*

---

* Okay, now, in 2015, *maybe* I'll admit that *possibly* there might

My mother's disdain for rules didn't sit well with a lot of people, particularly those who ran the governments of small countries.

In 1998 we were on vacation in the Caribbean, off of the island of Dominica. The captain of our boat* made a slight geographical mistake and accidentally dropped anchor in a designated nature preserve. We had no idea that this beautiful setting was a preserve or we never would have stopped there for lunch. We're sitting on the deck having lunch and all of a sudden we see these little tender boats filled with men in uniforms who were carrying guns . . . which they were pointing at us.

The highest-ranking officer on one of the tender boats got on a loudspeaker and shouted at us, "Move the boat! Move the boat or you will all be arrested immediately!" We started shaking in our flip-flops and putting our hands in the air, having no idea why any of this was happening. Everyone was terrified except my mother. She saw this as an opportunity for adventure and excitement and possibly some TV news face time: a triple play! She grabbed her camera and began filming, all the while screaming at them through a bullhorn, "This boat is private property. You are not allowed to board." I've got scenes of *Mid-*

---

have been a slight chance I was in a room with someone who was smoking pot and could have gotten a contact high from him. Maybe. But I still stand by the fact that I was trying to make donuts at 2:00 a.m. because I was hungry when the grease fire ignited in the kitchen. Coulda happened; anything's possible. But that's as far as I'm going to go.

* In the world of cruises, *boat* is a dirty word. As our captain explained to my mother, "Boats sink; ships don't." To which my mother replied, "What was the *Titanic,* a fucking boat?"

night Express playing in my head and she's turning to her friend, Phyllis, telling her to go put on a cover-up because she won't like how her tan lines look in the footage.

Eventually, as the tender boats got closer, I started explaining to my mother the gravity of the situation. She kept insisting that the men could not legally board the boat. I kept insisting that legally they could do whatever the fuck they wanted. At this point I took the camera from her and locked it in a closet; and then I lured her into her stateroom by saying that her lipstick was smudged, and promptly locked her inside. I left her in there until the Dominica Polizia and our captain did what they needed to do to resolve the mess.

As the police were finishing up, my mother escaped from her stateroom. Apparently, in the time we had kept her belowdecks, she had come up with another strategy and now raced up the stairs: "I'm writing an article for *Travel & Leisure* and I'm going to make sure your island gets bad reviews and low marks for hospitality."

The police stared at her like she was a crazy woman (which I can't say was inaccurate) and said nothing, as they had a limited command of English. Once I explained to my mother that we were in the wrong and that we had accidentally moored in a nature preserve, she said, "They should have put up a sign. In New York they put up signs for everything!" The next thing you know, it's photo ops and Bee Pins for la Polizia de Dominica!

Then there was the great Costa Rica incident. A few years ago Costa Rica was one of the hottest new vacation spots in the world. It was like South Beach with fewer Spanish-speaking people. And since my mother liked to be as trendy and current as possible, that's where we went on our annual vacation. Everything was great—the hotel, the weather, the people—until it was time to leave and come home.

When we were leaving Costa Rica we all checked in for our various flights out of the small jungle airport. Some of us were flying to Los Angeles, some to London, and my mother was flying back to New York, unaccompanied, which we rarely let her do. Even though we went to the airport together, our flights were at different times. My flight left in mid-afternoon; my mother's flight, the last one out, left two hours later. As Cooper and I got on our plane, she hugged us good-bye, and everything seemed fine.

Now for some backstory: Because my mother was in show business and worked under a stage name, her passport had two names on it, Joan Rosenberg and "aka Joan Rivers." This is legal and normal, no problem. When she checked in at the airport counter in Costa Rica, there was no problem, and they gave her a boarding pass. She got through immigration with no problem. I was already en route home and assumed she would get on her plane, no problem. When I got off in Dallas to change planes, however, I checked my phone and saw there was a message from her. Whenever any message from my mother began "Let me just start by saying everything is fine and I don't want you to be upset in case you hear what happened," I knew immediately not only that there was a problem, but there was a big problem. (Whenever she led with the end of the story first, I knew the story wasn't going to be good.) I wasn't concerned; I was apoplectic. I knew she was physically all right, because I'd heard her voice, but I could only imagine what she'd done.

Turns out when she went to board the plane, the local airline ticket agent wouldn't let her on because the name on the passport and the name on the boarding pass didn't match. So she showed them the passport with both names. The person at the gate didn't care. She showed it to the other ticket agent; they didn't care. So, rather than asking for a supervisor, what's the first thing she did? Rush the gate to get on the plane. She runs up the ramp and onto the aircraft to try to find the pilot, so *he* could explain to the ticket agent that Joan Rivers and Joan Rosenberg were the same person. At this point we now have violated many FAA rules and have an international incident on our hands. The pilot (and all the other passengers) vouched for her, but by this time she had pissed off the security officials and the people on the ground so much that they took her and her luggage off the plane. They not only removed her and her luggage from the airplane but they removed them from the airport altogether.

Being resourceful, she finds a car and drives to another airport in a bigger city and figures she'll try her luck there. Fortunately, the gate agents there did recognize her and were not only able to get her on a plane and get her out of the country, but they were eager to do so. (Somehow they managed to "find" an open seat on a sold-out flight to New York on the day after New Year's holiday. Imagine that!)

Dear readers, right about now you're probably thinking, "So, Melissa, how did your mother spend the six hours in the car going from the little airport to the big airport?" She spent it doing what any reasonable, sane, thoughtful person who had just created an international incident would do. She went on social media and began trash-talking the airlines, the personnel, and the inept immigration officers at the airport in Costa Rica. Figuring everyone knew she was Joan Rosenberg aka Joan Rivers, comedian, she thought this was quite funny. Apparently the government of Costa Rica did not. There was never a formal "you are not welcome in this country anymore" letter sent, but the next time we tried to book a trip to Costa Rica, there was not a hotel room to be found. In the entire country. 'Nuff said.

#joanriversgetoutanddon'tcomeback

Ivy Day

I GRADUATED FROM the University of Pennsylvania in 1989. Over graduation weekend, three notable individuals are invited to speak: one at graduation, one at the baccalaureate ceremony, and one at Ivy Day, where every graduating class places a commemorative stone or brick on the campus. The Ivy Day speaker is usually voted on by the graduating seniors, and that person's speech is the first event of the weekend. My mother was chosen by my class to share some thoughts with us on Ivy Day. It's amazing how, all these years later, much of what she said still holds true. With great pride I share with you her speech:

So this is Ivy Day, or as I call it Poison Ivy Day. I'm a little disappointed, because when they asked me to speak at graduation, I thought they meant graduation. I thought I'd be toasted with champagne and have my picture in *Time* magazine wearing a black cap and gown to match my roots. And that I'd be receiving a degree. It was even printed in the paper that I was going to get one, and then they said I wasn't getting the degree . . . then I was . . . and then I wasn't—it's a situation several of you seniors can relate to.

Anyhow, typical of my luck, Mike Wallace and Digby Baltzell and I end up talking one mile away from Franklin Field, thinking, "God forbid, they would make me plant that stupid ivy and how it will ruin a sixty-dollar manicure."

I will admit that when President Hackney called me, all I heard him say was something about Ivy Day being a big tradition and [he] mentioned something about there being a large stone involved. Being a JAP, I figured at best it would be a diamond and at worst an opal. I should have caught on that there wasn't any gift involved when, after hanging up, it occurred to me that President Hackney had called collect. "But no," I said to myself, "Joan, don't judge Sheldon Hackney too harshly. He's doing a fine job considering he thinks he's at Penn State."

Anyhow, this morning, Shelly—I can call him Shelly now 'cause my daughter passed everything—explained to me that each class plants ivy by a building that's marked by the Ivy Stone, and he said, "Joan, it's a real honor to be asked to speak on Ivy Day. Ignore the rumor that Morton Downey Jr. turned it down."

So here we are, all set to plant the Class of 1989's little bit of wildlife and let's pray Exxon doesn't come around and destroy it. As we come together today, I can't help but look out and see the faces of smiling parents. And I know what they're all thinking: "Thank God, I don't have to shell out $18,500 a year for tuition anymore." And I see all the seniors smiling. And I know that they're thinking: "Now that my parents don't have to pay $18,500 for tuition anymore, maybe they can buy me a $37,000 BMW." Now I look again at the faces of the parents and they aren't smiling anymore.

Today we join together to begin three days that will be filled with laughter, joy, and suddenly nostalgia. I personally can't believe, as a parent, just how fast all this has happened. It seems like yesterday that my husband and I were talking to Melissa about choosing a college. Since we came from California, you have to realize what a difficult evening that was. You see, in California, we look at higher education differently. To us, a higher education is anything after you stop coloring. The only culture that you find out there is in yogurt. In LA, their idea of an essential question is "How tan am I?" Los Angeles is not smart. I hate it. I hate it.

And yet despite our origins, I stand before you as the mother of a young woman who's about to graduate from a fine college. I am so proud that my daughter has come here and has had the privilege of spending four years on this campus. I see her out there now, smiling despite the fact that her history professor almost didn't accept her thesis, "Oliver North: Guys Just Want to Have Fun." And I wonder if she realizes, or if any of you graduating seniors realize, what it means to get a degree that says it's from the University of Pennsylvania? It means a lot and will for the rest of your lives.

Because Melissa's father and I knew that a good education was important, we were very picky as to where she went. So we came east and took the college tour. First, we toured Bennington, and I was shocked at the tuition. Believe me, you could run South Korea for a year for what it costs at that place. We went to look over Williams, where the most popular course was How to Speak to the Servants Without Using Your Facial Muscles. And last of all, we visited Brown and sat through a philosophy class, where they discussed "If a tree falls in the forest and nobody is around to hear it fall, does anyone give a damn?" Luckily, Melissa wanted, and was accepted at, Penn.

And now it's four years later, and this campus holds so many memories for me, as it does all the parents. Remember the first day we brought our children here? We unpacked them, helped put their new books away, and then left so that they could sneak out to sell those books to buy ripped jeans and compact discs. I have so many memories. The memory of the coed bathrooms, the memory of the bookstore with the condom machine, the memory of my first nervous breakdown, when I realized I was putting my daughter into this environment. And then there are the other memories. The first football game Melissa and I went to here: Penn versus Harvard. I climbed up, up, up, up to sit in those god-awful bleachers. Just when you think the game is over, the clock stops again. Melissa bet on Penn. I bet on which of the cheerleaders didn't have a nose job.

In these four years, I think my happiest moment

came in the middle of Melissa's sophomore year, when I realized that my daughter, my baby, was becoming an academic. We were waiting for a table at the Garden, talking about American literature, and in the two and a half hours it took to get the maitre d's eye, Melissa spoke about Willa Cather. She talked about Willa Cather's tone, her use of alliteration, her ideas, her primary philosophy, and never once did she mention that Willa Cather was gay. That's when I knew my daughter was getting a great education. Boring but great.

And now that these four years are drawing to a close, they have asked me, out of desperation, to provide a lofty message for you graduates that can help you be happy in real life. Well, I would love to say, "You are our hope for the future and you are going to go forth and make everything bright and right in a wonderful world," but I think I'll pass on those chestnuts. Instead, I'd like to tell you the truth as I see it. Look to your left, look to your right, look all around you. Because, seniors, this is as good as it's going to get for a long, long time. Whether you know it or not, you've all had it easy up to now.

You've been pampered, you've been supported, and you actually knew where you were going to be the next day and what would happen to you there. Now it's time to go out into a world where not everyone is a 3.5, where not everyone has a twenty-one-inch waist, and a lot of people think the National Rifleman's [sic] Association is a swell bunch of guys, into the real world, where people lie, cheat, and steal. A world so

terrifying that stoves come with bars on their windows and where some think that Washington, DC,
stands for "District of Crack."

On the bright side, you're entering a world of
choices. I've decided to give you some tips on how to
make the right ones. Now, a lot of you are probably
thinking, "Who is she, that old tramp, to give advice?"
Well, who am I? I'm a mother, a television personality,
and a woman who believes if you eat standing up over
the sink, those calories don't count. But more than
that, I like to think of myself as a survivor in a business that's tough to survive in, and because of that, I
have plenty of advice to give you. Plus, as I've got the
microphone and you don't, here it is.

If this were a movie, there would now be a big
crack of thunder, a bolt of lightning, and I would be
standing here as a blonde Charlton Heston, holding
two heavy stone tablets, that would hold the "Ten
Commandments for Graduating Seniors." I don't
want to be didactic. Let's call these the "Ten Suggestions," and as we all want to get out and have fun,
with no disrespect to Moses, let's not make them ten,
let's make them seven. I picked that number in honor
of the age of Cher's new boyfriend.

My first suggestion would be: Plan to fail. If you're
lucky, you'll fail early. Failure was the best thing that
ever happened to me. It will be for you, too. Not only
did each failure in my life teach me something, it made
me stronger and moved me one step closer to success.

During the first two years I was in the business,

I was fired from every job I got. What did this teach me? To believe in myself when no one else does.

A few years later, I was the only member of the Second City comedy group not to be signed by an agency. What did I learn from that? Maybe I was meant to work alone.

My latest failure was being publicly fired from a national television show. What did I learn from that? That even at my age, I was still able to call on energies and strengths I had long thought had vanished with easy living. The point is, look at failure as something positive. Jane Fonda doesn't have a lock on "No pain, no gain." You deal with it, you make a joke, and you put it in perspective, and move on.

The second suggestion is don't be proud. If you think the world is waiting for you now that you've graduated, you're wrong. To quote Kermit, "It ain't easy being green." And you're green. No one is waiting for you. So don't sit around and figure "I'm from Wharton, I'm from Penn. I'm going to get that dream job or else wait for the perfect opportunity." Remember, "Pride goeth before a fall." Just ask me.

Try any path you can, go through any door that opens. Don't wait for the right moment, because right moments usually come out of wrong ones. Let me give you an example. Barbra Streisand and I started out together. She is such an individual, one of a kind. She could not get arrested. She tried everything to get jobs, but nothing happened for months and months. Finally, in desperation, she sneaked into an audition for *The Sound of Music,* where they were casting the role of the sixteen-year-old blonde ingénue. You know, an impossibly sweet blonde, nomadic, Aryan, blue-eyed . . . How can I describe her? A Nazi. Streisand didn't get the job, but somebody in the back of the auditorium heard her audition. He suggested she try singing in nightclubs—any nightclub, for starters. When she did, she was offered the role in the Broadway play *I Can Get It for You Wholesale,* which led to the lead in *Funny Girl.* She wasn't too proud, and as a result she became a star. And from that day on, that bitch has not returned my calls, but you get the idea: Start in anywhere. Just remember that a lot of people who are out getting coffee today will be Ivan Boesky tomorrow.

Suggestions three and four on how to get along in real life are about love and money, and if you don't think the two are tied together, try spending three weeks in Hollywood.

First of all, money. Jean Paul Getty once said, "If you know how much money you have, you don't have enough." I agree with him. Get out there, work hard, and thank God we're living in a country where the sky is still the limit and the stores are open late. Now, I come from the Flower Power generation. And yes, you can be happy without money. But, believe me, it helps. Money is wonderful. That's why Abbie Hoffman, at the end of his life, was getting a lecture fee of $8,000 to tell college kids how money meant nothing. Now, how to get it. Don't go looking for it. Find the work you'd pay to do and eventually people will pay you for it. Handsomely. If you're in a job where you're just hanging around for a paycheck or gazing at the clock all afternoon, you're in the wrong place and nothing good is going to happen there. Trust me. I don't think the Pope ever asked for a job description.

Now, love, money's first cousin. Look for love and when you find it, grab it with both hands. And if it isn't there at the moment, don't be discouraged; it comes to everybody. Look at Princess Anne of England: a husband and a boyfriend and a face that is a real twelve-bagger.

But when love comes, should you buy a real sofa, or a sectional, so you can split it up if it doesn't work out? Get the sofa and go for the gold. Don't just live together; get married. Marriage is just like living together, but better, because you get a lot of presents. And marriage will give you a haven and stability. You create a unit. When the music stops, you'll find it's an "us versus them" world, and your only true ally will be your spouse.

My fifth suggestion is about success, which is the thing you most crave. I hope you all get it. Let me tell you what success means. It doesn't mean that everyone will love you. I believe it was Thoreau who said, "There is no success without envy until you're dead." So the more successful you become, the fewer people will encourage you and cheer you on, and the more successful you become, the fewer people you'll trust. Success isolates you. But that's not bad, because if you've made it on your own, it gives you the chance to say, "I did it. No one helped me." That's only two sentences, and that's good because success is a short-lived phenomenon that's never to be trusted. Enjoy it for the moment and then get back to work. Never forget that work is the reason you became successful.

Suggestion six is grammatical. Use your education. Remember always: It's not *who* you know; it's *whom*.

Last suggestion—and I think I can say this for all the parents here. Don't think just because you've gotten your degree, your childhood is over. As long as you've got a parent left, you can always be a child to someone. The light is in the window.

You can always come home. For two days or two weeks or two years— although, I think that would be pushing it.

Wow! I don't think I've ever spoken so long without breaking for a commercial. So here's mine.

This is an incredible day for all of you. And, kidding aside, it has cost each of you something to be here. I want to close by acknowledging one graduating senior, Melissa Rosenberg, who has, believe me, earned this degree. That she made it through at all with what has churned around her for the last four years is remarkable. That she made it through as a talented, sane, nice person is my greatest source of pride. I was asked to speak today because I'm funny, caustic, and cheap. That's not the reason I accepted. I came because I wanted to pay tribute, in public, to my daughter, to her friends, and to the institution which supported them, nurtured them, and please, God, educated them. I think that means that Penn has taught you to see, to hear, to smell, taste, and touch. Do it, let it happen. One of my favorite lines from the theater is in *Mame,* when she says, "Life is a banquet, but most sons of bitches are starving to death." Don't let that be you. The best to all of you. Thank you.

P.S. She's *still* pissed that the only one who didn't receive an honorary degree is the Ivy Day speaker. Emmy-schmemmy, she never got past that. "I paid my own fucking way out here and I don't get a degree? Melissa, whom do I talk to about this?"

Speaking of My Mother . . .

THE FIRST PUBLIC appearance I made after my mother's death was at *The Hollywood Reporter*'s Women in Entertainment Breakfast in December 2014. My mother was being honored at the event, and I was asked to say a few words. Here is the text of my remarks:

> First of all, thank you all so much for inviting me to be here this morning. Before we start, I'd like to point out that it's a little overwhelming being in a room with the most beautiful, successful, powerful women in Hollywood. But Angelina [Jolie], don't be intimidated. I'm really quite easy and accessible.
>
> For me, this has been an interesting three months and six days—not that I'm counting—to say the least.
>
> When Janice [Min] asked if I would say a few words today, I was overwhelmed. Not just because it is the first time I'm speaking in tribute to my mother, but because every single person in this room could hire me, and a few have actually fired me. (You know

who you are, and I'm not trying to make you feel guilty, although I *am* an orphan.) Also, let's be honest, no one is actually listening to anything anyone is saying because we are all too busy looking at each other's bags, shoes, and jewelry. At least *I* am—my mother taught me that cleanliness isn't next to godliness; shallowness is.

A few weeks ago at the *Glamour* Women of the Year Awards, Amy Schumer spoke about my mother. She hit on something that actually applies to everyone in the room, and that was that my mother was brave. I had never thought of that, but when I look back at her life, I truly think that might be the best word to apply to her.

From the time she was a small child, my mom took risks. At eight years old, she went into her parents' living room and took her picture off the piano and sent it to MGM. In her mind, clearly this little girl was a star. So, she sent the photo, frame and all. Needless to say, my grandmother, a formidable woman herself, was not pleased. It was a fifty-dollar frame.

At ten, my mom was sent home from Camp Kinnykaknick, for organizing a strike—she didn't like the way the drama counselor cast *Snow White and the Seven Dwarfs*. They had given her the part of Dopey, and she was pissed she had no lines. She said she "understood her character and that Dopey's aggressive silence would be seen as an affront to Happy, Grumpy, and Doc." My grandparents were called and told to come and get her and that they had raised, and

I quote, "the next Hitler or Eleanor Roosevelt," they weren't sure which, but to come and get her. And this was a Jewish camp.

At seventy-eight she began hosting *Fashion Police,* the funniest, edgiest, possibly most controversial show on TV, and last week, at eighty-one, she was posthumously nominated for a Grammy* for her book *Diary of a Mad Diva,* which had this disclaimer:

> *This diary was written to the best of Joan Rivers's memory. As such, some of the events may not be 100 percent . . . or even 5 percent factually correct. Miss Rivers is, after all, 235 years old, and frequently mistakes her daughter, Melissa, for the actor Laurence Fishburne.*
>
> *Miss Rivers wrote this diary as a comedic tome, not unlike* Saving Private Ryan *or* The Bell Jar. *While Miss Rivers doesn't really like skinny models and actresses, she doesn't actually believe that they're all bulimics and they all carry buckets instead of purses. Similarly, she doesn't really think that all Germans are anti-Semitic Nazi sympathizers, that all Mexican Americans tunneled in across the border, that all celebrities are drug addicts, shoplifters, or closet cases, or that Noah built his ark with non-union labor.*
>
> *Miss Rivers does, however, believe that anyone who takes anything in this book seriously is*

---

* Which she won.

an idiot. And she says if anyone has a problem
with that they can feel free to call her lawyer,
Clarence Darrow.

My mother was fearless. I don't mean she didn't
have any fears. I mean that even though she was only
five two, she stood tall and walked through them.
That is what made her such a brilliant performer. She
was willing to say what others were thinking and too
frightened to admit. She made fun of herself first and
foremost, which gave her the right to joke about others.

She never apologized for a joke, and no topic was
taboo, which sometimes made men uncomfortable.
And she was fine with that. She was working in a
man's world, and if men were offended or uncomfortable by some joke she told, she'd say, "Oh, grow up!"

Truth be told, my mother never thought of herself as a woman working in a man's world. She just
thought of herself as a comic and knew she just had
to be funnier than *everyone else,* be it man, woman,
child, straight, gay, single, married, or "bi-curious,"
whatever the hell that is. She just wanted to do her
job, and that was to make people laugh.

For the last few months, there has been tribute after tribute to my mom. She has been called
everything from a legend to a trailblazer, to a bitch.
It's hard for me to really think of her as any of those
things, because to me she was just my mother. I guess
it is true that most of us women who all have a powerful voice in our respective fields wouldn't be here if it
weren't for that brave little girl who sent her photo in.

If my mother were here this morning, she'd not only be grateful and proud; she'd be thrilled. She'd be sitting at the table beaming . . . while very discreetly shoving croissants and silverware into her purse.

On behalf of my mother, thank you so much for this wonderful honor.

"Melissa, into every life darkness must fall. None of us are spared from pain and suffering. But your blessings far outweigh your difficulties. You have a roof over your head, food on your table, a healthy body, a healthy mind, and a healthy child. But far more important than all of that—you have fabulous shoes."

The End

===

September 3, 2014

BACK TO MOUNT Sinai Hospital. My mother has been in an irreversible coma for a week, and the time has come to say good-bye. I have invited the people she meant the most to, and who meant the most to her, to come for one last visit.

For hours, friends from all over the world came in to spend a little time at her bedside. Some laughed, some cried—it was like going to the Broadway show *Cats*—yet they all managed to hit the deli platters I had set up across the hall pretty hard. (Apparently, overwhelming grief creates blood sugar issues.)

I was focused on making sure that the people who were coming to say good-bye all had time with my mother. Keeping the line moving was a blessed distraction, and I went into work mode and felt useful, instead of helpless, as I had felt for the past seven days.

After everyone had said their good-byes and gone,

Cooper went in to spend a few minutes with his grandmother. He held her hand and cried and just sat with her. They had put a cot in her room so I could lie next to her that last night, and Cooper lay down next to me until he was tired enough so he could fall asleep in the other room that the hospital had so generously provided for us.

I slept on the cot next to my mother's bed that night, with some of the lights still on and the TV blasting, just the way she liked it.

In the morning, when it was time to remove the ventilator, she was surrounded by those who loved her most, and whom she loved most. I lay in the bed and held her for a while, and after a few hours she was finally gone. I didn't have to tell her I loved her; she knew. She didn't have to tell me she loved me; I knew.

ALTHOUGH MY MOTHER joked how she wanted her memorial service to be in her book *I Hate Everyone . . . Starting with Me,* we never actually discussed what she might want. When it was actually time to plan her memorial, I tried to honor what I imagined her wishes would be, fully and completely—a service that was elegant, funny, and just enough "showbiz" to make it feel like a great old MGM movie.

"When I die (and yes, Melissa, that day will come; and yes, Melissa, everything's in your name), I want my funeral to be a big showbiz affair with lights, cameras, action…
I want Craft services, I want paparazzi and I want publicists making a scene! I want it to be Hollywood all the way.
I don't want some rabbi rambling on; I want Meryl Streep crying, in five different accents. I don't want a eulogy;
I want Bobby Vinton to pick up my head and sing "Mr. Lonely." I want to look gorgeous, better dead than I do alive. I want to be buried in a Valentino gown and I want Harry Winston to make me a toe tag.
And I want a wind machine so that even in the casket my hair is blowing just like Beyoncé's."

—JOAN RIVERS
I HATE EVERYONE… STARTING WITH ME

ORDER OF SERVICE

NEW YORK CITY GAY MEN'S CHORUS

Opening Prayers
RABBI JOSHUA DAVIDSON

Musical Interlude
AUDRA MCDONALD

Tribute
DEBORAH NORVILLE

Reminiscences
MARGIE STERN
CINDY ADAMS
MELISSA RIVERS

Musical Interlude
HUGH JACKMAN

Closing Prayers

PIPES & DRUMS OF THE EMERALD SOCIETY,
NEW YORK CITY POLICE DEPARTMENT

Acknowledgments

=====

FIRST AND FOREMOST, I have to thank Larry Amoros. You have guided me through this process, kept me laughing, and listened when I needed an ear. What can I say other than I love you beyond words.

I'd also like to thank Suzanne O'Neill, my editor, who ventured into the crazy waters of this process with me, and kept it all afloat. You are a brave, brave woman. Also the team at Crown Archetype: Molly Stern, Tricia Boczkowski, Tammy Blake, Julie Cepler, and Jenni Zellner.

My amazing agent and friend, CC Hirsch. How you put up with all of us day after day, I have no clue. My literary agent, Cait Hoyt, who believed in me and this project from the beginning, and laughed at all my jokes.

Michael Karlin—how do I ever say thank you for everything you are to me and Cooper? I can't.

Ken Browning and Marc Chamlin, for reading all of the fine print and being sounding boards extraordinaire.

David Dangle and the JMAM team, for keeping my mother's beloved jewelry business alive.

And of course, the people who have been there

through it all: Jocelyn Pickett, Graham Reed, Melody McCoy, Margie and Michael Stern, the Waxler family, Michael and Caroline Levitt, the Tilden family, Scott Currie, Judy Katz, Henry Edwards, Robert Higdon, Pete Hathaway, Karl and Deborah Wellner, Blaine Trump, Amy Rosenblum, Countess Sondes, Sue Solomon, Deborah Freid and family, Laura Brau and family, Jaimie and Michael Geller, Andrew Krasny, Beth and Jon Kean, Kyle and Emme Kozloff, Chris and Marla Ahearn, Lawrence Kaplan, all of my Penn family, Allie Mays, Team MacClean, Susi Cohen, Shauna Somers Greene, Chuck Labella, Charles Cook, Phil Gurin, Peggy Harris, Gary Lamberson, Adele Fass, Raymond Rosario, Gavin de Becker, Elizabeth Much, Howard Bragman, Gary Snegaroff, Lisa Bacon, Kelly Osbourne, George Kotsiopoulos, Giuliana Rancic, Tony Tripoli, Tom McNamara and the studio A crew, Vera Vanatko, Norma Hernandez, Analie Berthel, Johanna Barrios, Gladys Villalobos, Merlita Eldiasti, Duagua Roberts, Angeles Beltran, Dr. David Scott May and Dr. David Kipper, and the eighth-grade Santa Monica Dragons lacrosse players, parents, and coaches.

To Ted Harbert for bringing my mother and me back to E!

To Bonnie Hammer for her amazing advice, both personal and professional.

To Cary Fetman for years of love.

To Sabrina Miller for being my sister, my friend, my confidante, and the rational side of my brain.

To Mark Rousso for loving me in spite of everything.

And to Cooper. You are the best thing that ever happened to me.